More
Duologues

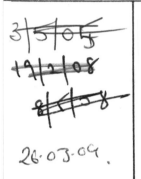

To Don Taylor and Ellen Dryden
'Thank you'

First published 2003
A & C Black Publishers Limited
37 Soho Square, London W1D 3QZ
www.acblack.com

© 2003 Eamonn Jones and Jean Marlow

ISBN 0-7136-6527-0

A CIP catalogue record for this book is available from
the British Library.

A & C Black uses paper produced with elemental chlorine-free
pulp, harvested from managed sustainable forests.

Typeset in 10pt on 12pt Sabon
Printed and bound in Great Britain by
Creative Print and Design (Wales), Ebbw Vale

Contents

Duologues for Two Men

Duologues for Two Women

Duologues for One Man and One Woman

Acknowledgements

We would like to say thank you to the actors, directors, producers, playwrights and organisations who have helped us with this book, including:

Alan Ayckbourn, David Carey of Central School of Speech and Drama, Frances Cuka, April De Angelis, Helen Fry, Bill Germano, Miles Gregory, Julian Holland, Tesni Hollands, Rona Laurie, Martin Phillips – librarian for Samuel French, John Quinlan, Carol Schroder, Brian Schwartz of Offstage Bookshop, Heather Stoney and Don Taylor.

Also students from the Actors' Theatre School who work-shopped these duologues.

And not forgetting our indefatigable Editors, Jessica Hodge and Katie Taylor.

Foreword

In addition to their work as actors and as Directors of the Actors' Theatre School, Jean Marlow and Eamonn Jones have a growing reputation as compilers of audition speeches and duologues. Indeed, whole shelves at Samuel French and at Brian Schwartz's Offstage Bookshop will soon be needed to accommodate their books! This new one, *More Duologues for all accents and ages* is a follow-up to their *Duologues for all accents and ages*, which appeared in 1997.

Today the duologue is being increasingly recognised in the professional theatre as an art form. One of the most successful and artistically satisfying productions in London's West End last year was Brian Friel's two-hander *Afterplay*. Duologues are also becoming more popular on tour and at fringe events. Amateur Dramatic Societies are always on the look-out for fresh ones to enter in Drama Festivals; too few have been chasing too many Festivals for too long.

As regards acting examinations, the Guildhall School of Music and Drama now includes duologues up to Grade 8 in its syllabus, and the London Academy of Music and Dramatic Art includes them up to Silver and Gold Medals. Teachers and drama tutors alike are sometimes quite desperate to find suitable scenes.

Jean Marlow and Eamonn Jones have provided strongly contrasted situations, styles, characters and moods in this selection. It should offer challenging opportunities to actors and students alike.

Rona Laurie
FGSM, LRAM, GODA, FRSA

More Duologues

An experimental hospital for the criminally insane . . .

Two men are sitting in a psychiatrist's office. One is a paperback crime writer, the other the psychiatrist himself – or is he? The journalist is persuaded to try on a strait jacket, just to see how it feels to be completely helpless. *Mindgame*, by Anthony Horowitz.

A Scottish Border farm of 1860 . . .

Each farm worker is hired on condition that he brings a female to work alongside him – if not his wife or daughter, then some girl he has hired at the Hiring Fair. *The Bondagers*, by Sue Glover.

A London Tally Shop in 1726 . . .

Mrs Tull has problems with her business and the whores are giving her a bad time. *Mother Clap's Molly House*, by Mark Ravenhill – developed with students from the London Academy of Music and Dramatic Art (LAMDA).

The above situations and their settings all demand very different styles of playing. They not only provide good entertainment but also excellent roles for Final Year Showcases.

In this new book, a companion to the original *Duologues for all accents and ages*, we've incorporated not only a variety of accents but also a range of different periods and styles. There are actors who feel uneasy with certain classical plays and won't even attempt them for fear of being 'found out'. They **learned** about them at drama school, but never had the opportunity to actually **perform** in them. An actor friend remembers being given a choice between taking part in a full-length production of *Iphigenia in Taurus* or Shakespeare's *The Merchant of Venice*. He chose *The Merchant* because he knew nothing about 'the Greeks' and felt they were 'best left alone'! Years after leaving drama school if anyone suggested him for Greek drama, or even Molière – 'Who's he, then?' – he'd panic completely. So we decided this was a problem that needed to be faced up to here and now, in this book.

Given a choice, most actors will pick out duologues with characters they feel at home with. This is understandable when it comes to the Final Showcase, examinations, or general auditions, but in classwork you have an opportunity to experiment, try out new ideas and make mistakes. Find out all you can about the period your scene was written in. See how the costume of that time affects movement and gesture. Learn how to speak blank verse with confidence. You may surprise yourself and find it easier than modern text!

Experiment with an accent or dialect you've never attempted before. Make a note of where the consonant and vowel changes occur and mark them in on your script. It's a good idea to build up your own collection of voice tapes – the ones you buy can be excellent but not always exactly what you're looking for and, if recorded out of doors with members of the public, are sometimes too broad and difficult to 'sort out', or overlaid with interference from street noises. We came across a tape not long ago containing, amongst others, a 'Liverpool' accent. The extract was recorded in a pub in Liverpool, but turned out to be the voice of a barmaid just over from Dublin!

Voice

The most important attribute of the actor is 'Voice'. **David Carey**, Principal Lecturer in Voice Studies at the Central School of Speech and Drama, has this to say:

Vocal expressivity
The voice is an integral part of the actor's art. In our contemporary digital age of computer graphics, sound cards, instant messaging and video conferencing, it is easy to take the spoken word for granted. But the human voice and its expressivity remain unique forms of communication which speak from the heart to the soul, and from the body to the mind. The actor has a responsibility to humanity to maintain the vitality and immediacy of this essential medium of expression.

To do this requires work. Work to realise our full vocal potential, and to achieve the expressive flexibility that will enable the actor to embody the full range of characters he or she may be asked to play in their professional lifetime. Muscular work and imaginative work. Muscular work to enable the voice to live in the whole body, to access the free and flexible breath which will empower the voice, to open up the totality of available pitch and resonance, to bring tone and skill to the articulators – tongue, lips and soft palate – which shape and enliven speech. Imaginative work to develop the emotional and intellectual connection to language, to link the inner life of a character to public expressivity, and to embody the author's text with courage and commitment. This is work that can be done throughout an actor's career – from first audition at drama school to final swan song on stage; for theatre performances, film cameos, voice-overs and the latest television soap opera. It is work that needs to be done **now**.

Facing up to the Classics

As in the first duologue book we have invited well-known playwrights, actors and directors to talk about scenes from plays they have either written, performed in or directed – paying particular attention to extracts from some of the earlier classics.

Theatre and television director **Don Taylor** directed his translation of *Antigone* for BBC Television in 1986:

Greek tragedies compress their subject matter into archetypal images of human behaviour. All the plays we have – a mere 31 out of what must have been many thousands written; Euripides alone is thought to have written more than a hundred, of which we have 17, and of Sophocles we have only seven – are concerned with the great themes and conflicts of human life. There are no little anecdote plays or character studies in Greek drama.

There is no point at all in playing them in any style remotely akin to modern naturalism. The actor needs to approach them more in the spirit of a great opera singer, a Callas or a Tito Gobbi, than a television or film actor. Passion is required and depth of feeling, from the first word to the last. All Greek drama is poetry, written in various forms of verse, and it has the intensity you would expect these styles to generate.

In the scenes between Creon and Haemon and Antigone and Ismene, some of the verses are laid out according to a verse form called stichomythia, which creates a dialogue between two characters – on odd occasions even three or including the chorus – by employing a pattern of exactly balanced single or two-line speeches, which can continue for several minutes. All Greek tragedies contain such passages. They usually express particularly dramatic moments of confrontation, and they often represent the dramatic highlights of the play, as in the scene between father and son, or Oedipus teasing out his fate from the Man from Corinth and the Old Shepherd. They must be played with great passion, but formally, well aware of the verse structure and movement, and with no attempt to smooth away the shape of the lines.

Naturalism has no part in Greek drama. The characters must always be realistically interpreted – there is a great and profound acting difference between the concepts of naturalism and realism –

but within the convention of poetic word-based acting. If you try to play a Greek character like someone from a soap opera or a film, you will fail. Use your voice as a musical instrument that conveys truth, and you might get somewhere near the summits that only the greatest actors succeed in climbing.

Miles Gregory is the Artistic Director and founder of the British Touring Shakespeare Company. In the last three years his productions have played to over 30,000 people, from London's West End to Dubai. He has also led workshops at the Globe Theatre, London and lectured on Shakespeare at the Universities of Cambridge, Exeter, Durham and Auckland. Here he talks about the extract from Shakespeare's *Twelfth Night*:

The character of Viola best embodies the extremes of love and loss that can be found in *Twelfth Night*. Tortured by the loss of her brother, in the lovelorn court of Orsino she finds a love that transcends her loss – loving a man who is himself lost in love. Viola has lost her brother, lost her gender, and finally loses herself to Orsino. Her hopeless, unspoken love for Orsino, and Orsino's voluble love for Olivia are at the heart of this scene.

Shakespeare has written this scene in what is known as blank verse (i.e. unrhymed poetry), or iambic pentameter. The term 'iambic pentameter' describes the rhythm of the words: iambic means that there are two beats to each section, the first unstressed, the second stressed ('*de-dum*'), and pentameter tells us that there are five sections to each line ('*de-dum de-dum de-dum de-dum de-dum*'). Each beat corresponds to a syllable – and it follows that there are normally ten syllables in a line.

There are many approaches to dealing with blank verse, but in my work with actors we focus on a few guidelines which use the metre to help in actual performance. Let's look at a sample couple of lines:

> Viola: Too **well** what **love** women to **men** may **owe**.
> In **faith** they **are** as **true** of **heart** as **we**.

You will notice that Shakespeare has written these lines so that the important words fall on stressed beats – usually the nouns, verbs and adjectives/adverbs. When only part of a word falls on a stress (like wo**men**), think of the whole word as stressed, and where there is no punctuation at the end of a line, do not take a breath, but use the last word as a springboard, carrying the sense over to the next line. Not every word should be given the same amount of emphasis – the choice is yours. Verse is normally spoken by 'high characters' like lovers and nobles, and can tell you a lot about the characters and circumstances of a scene. The more passionate a scene, the less the verse sticks to ten syllables a line: the turmoil of the emotion is reflected in uneven lines of verse.

The most important thing when speaking verse is not to sound unnatural or to 'sing' it too much, a style known as 'declaiming' the verse. Try and fit the verse to your own speaking style: the more natural and real you can make it sound, the better.

When I was rehearsing *Twelfth Night* for the Westminster Theatre, we found that this scene was an emotional and dramatic climax for the characters. It builds in tension until Orsino's passionate explosion on 'What dost thou know?' Ironically, Viola knows far more about love than Orsino. Her own experience with Olivia has taught her that love must be reciprocated if it is to come to fruition. She knows 'Too well what love women to men may owe' – and for the first time Orsino listens. Viola, play-acting a man with the feelings of a woman, has painfully found out what constitutes real love. With her newfound understanding, she truly is 'all the daughters of her father's house,/And all the brothers too . . .'

Helen Fry has directed many period plays in London, national tours of Shakespeare with her company Gloriana, and has also worked abroad and in repertory. She recently directed a season of new writing at the Gielgud Theatre. Here she talks about the extract from Molière's *School for Wives* and Farquhar's *The Recruiting Officer*.

School for Wives
Molière was a 'complete' man of the theatre: touring all over France, writing, directing, acting and producing. His early plays were nearly all farces, with characters derived from the *commedia dell'arte*. Take time to find out about this, as it is important to find an appropriate physicality for your character: how do they stand, move, gesture? Indeed, the character of Arnolphe (originally played by Molière himself) owes much to the stock character Pantalone, a wealthy old man who believes that everything can be bought and

can't keep his hands to himself. Here he is obsessed with his desire not to be cuckolded and there's a lot of comic mileage in letting the lid off his control in the asides. Agnes needs to be played with simplicity and genuine innocence: she has been brought up in isolation from the world and is, as the scene shows, gullible and comically ignorant.

You will notice that the play is written in alexandrines – 12 syllables to each line, rhyming in couplets. The aim is to be as natural as possible and not let the rhythm of the verse and the rhyming couplets take over. As a guideline, go from punctuation mark to punctuation mark – if there's no punctuation at the end of a line, you must carry the sense over – do not pause or take a breath. A full stop in the middle of a line indicates a change of thought and a renewed energy. Where characters share a line, don't pause before you come in – keep the rhythm going. This puts the characters under pressure and heightens the comedy, especially when it arises out of a misunderstanding. For instance, when Arnolphe asks if Agnes' visitor took anything from her, she is embarrassed and admits, yes, he did. Arnolphe goes through torment that it is her virginity that has been taken, when in fact, it was a ribbon. This scene is full of jokes like this, so keep going through to the punchlines.

The Recruiting Officer
After Charles II was restored to the throne in 1660, returning with his court from exile in France, there was a huge explosion of energy in the theatre (which had been banned under the commonwealth). Not only did women now appear on the English stage, as in France, for the first time, but Molière's plays were plundered for their comic themes and situations.

Like many of the earlier Restoration comedies, *The Recruiting Officer* is about lovers' intrigues, marriage and money. You really need to research the period and make sure you understand the text – the language can be quite complex, with long sentences and subclauses and you need to be on top of it. This takes a lot of energy. Make sure you always have enough breath support to carry you through with ease – you must be like a swan – all poise and control, while paddling hard out of sight. These comedies are exactly that, fun: characters revel in playing games with and on each other. Don't forget they are also based in reality: they confide in each other and take risks in the hope that a new love interest will prove to be 'the one'. The character of Sergeant Kite in the opening scene is based on Farquhar's own experiences as a recruiting officer in Shrewsbury. And in the later scene, Melinda confides in her maid, Lucy about her visit to a famous fortune teller in town – who is of course Kite in disguise.

April De Angelis' most recent plays include *The Positive Hour* and *A Warwickshire Testimony*, produced by the Royal Shakespeare Company at the Other Place, Stratford-upon-Avon. Her latest play *A Laughing Matter* opened at the Royal National Theatre in 2002. It is set in 1773 at the Theatre Royal Drury Lane and is described as an irreverent version of events in the life of Actor Manager David Garrick, his wife and his mistress, the Irish actress Peg Woffington – and a new play called *She Stoops To Conquer*.

Garrick has left Peg, despite the fact that he has been besotted with her. However, in a world where respectability means survival he has chosen not to stay with her, but to choose a more respectable wife. Previously Peg has turned down an offer of a handsome living from an admirer to be with Garrick. The personal and professional are closely intertwined. In leaving her and her world behind Garrick has also chosen to side with a different kind of theatre, the theatre of polite sentiment as opposed to the old values of the bawdy Restoration theatre.

It is important to find out as much as you can about the characters you are playing. Peg Woffington and David Garrick were, of course, real-life characters. Their relationship is well documented in biographies; they had lived together for a while – Garrick always complained that Peg wasted tea leaves! (I read a lot into that: she carefree, sensuous; he more careful, controlled.) Peg had a reputation for having many lovers, and although Garrick finally asked her to marry him, he quickly had second thoughts.

The actors in *A Laughing Matter* found the research into such historical material invaluable when preparing their parts, and as a result brought the scene to life wonderfully with Peg's fiery nature and Garrick's canny incisiveness.

Working Today in Professional Theatre

Alan Ayckbourn, Artistic Director of the Stephen Joseph Theatre, is one of our busiest playwrights and directors. Here he talks about *GamePlan* and *FlatSpin* – two of the new plays we are using in this book – under the overall title of *Damsels in Distress*, and explains the advantages of working with a 'company'.

Recently, as with so many regional companies, we had begun to rely more and more on actors visiting us, short term, for one or maybe two productions. Spot-casting in this way has its advantages. But what you lose, of course, is the true company. The moment when a group of individual (sometimes highly individual) actors through familiarity, growing confidence and trust in each other forms that most unique of all theatrical achievements – a shared 'corporate' identity. The individuality remains – but the sum of the separate parts has generated something greater and stronger.

Personally I try to put together companies consisting of people that I like, and trust to luck that this common bond will prove a strong enough glue to hold the elements together. It was with this principle in mind that I put together the 2001 Scarborough summer company of seven.

I had written the company two plays, *GamePlan* and *FlatSpin*. Both were really entirely separate, linked by an identical cast size and the same set. The overall title I selected for them both – *Damsels in Distress* – did, though, reflect the fact that both plays were about women who in one way or other had found themselves up against it in the modern world.

GamePlan rehearsed and opened successfully and, in what seemed like no time at all (about seven or eight weeks), we were midway through rehearsals for *FlatSpin*. It was then that the 'company' effect began to take hold, as it had done in the past. As the group developed and consolidated, so I began to get the desire to write something more for them. Mid-morning, during a rehearsal, I announced that there could – possibly be – if they didn't mind – though it wasn't in any of their contracts – so if they *did* mind of course, then I wouldn't mind – there could be a third play for them to do . . . Rather stunned, they agreed. I don't, in retrospect, think it was much of a choice for them, though.

We opened *FlatSpin* on a Tuesday. I went home rather prematurely from the first-night party; the following day I started work on what was to become *RolePlay*. Just over a week later, on the following Thursday, I presented the cast with their new script. *Damsels in Distress* was now officially a trilogy. Same set, same actors but a totally fresh set of characters.

Although the plays can be seen individually and in any order, this last written piece by happy coincidence brought the entire company onstage together in a seven-handed scene. A fitting finale, I thought.

Frances Cuka, Royal Shakespeare and Royal National Theatres player, worked with Joan Littlewood's Theatre Workshop. Here she talks about how she came to play the much coveted role of 'Jo' in Shelagh Delaney's *A Taste of Honey*.

One Friday, long ago, I found myself on the Central Line on my way to the Theatre Royal Stratford East, or Theatre Workshop as it was more commonly known. The director of the theatre was the great Joan Littlewood, one of the most innovative directors the theatre has ever known. I had worked with her once before, an exciting and unnerving experience, and I was on my way there to read and work on a new play which was going into rehearsal almost immediately. The theatre was stony broke at the time, and the play had only five in the cast. It was called *A Taste of Honey*. Its author, Shelagh Delaney, was a young girl who had been to the theatre once in her life, and thought she could do better.

We found the play far too long and needing a great deal of tidying and tightening up, but it had vibrancy and freshness too. I wanted desperately to play 'Jo', a wonderful part for a young actress, though I was worried what my mother would think of it, with its themes of prostitution, child abuse, homosexuality, and pregnancy from a black lover.

I was the only one reading 'Jo', though several actors were alternating the other parts. That did not stop me being wary, however, as Joan could brutally change her mind. She wanted us back on Saturday morning to read again. Afterwards, Joan said that she was still undecided about the casting, and would ring us over the weekend. Rehearsals would start on Tuesday at ten o'clock.

All weekend I was glued to the phone, but no call came from Joan. All Monday I waited, but nothing. By Tuesday I was in a rage, and went down to Stratford steaming! Ten o'clock came and not a soul had arrived. They all swanned in at ten-thirty. I rushed up to Joan and shrieked, 'Am I playing this part or not?' Very gently she said, 'Yes, of course you are,' as to an idiot child. I've always had a sneaking suspicion that if I hadn't turned up that morning, she might have rung someone else.

We had no Stage Management and set our own props. Murray Melvin did all the cues in the first act, as he wasn't on, and Avis Bunnage and the Wardrobe Mistress sang the children's song offstage in the second act. The subject matter ensured that we had packed houses. We had two fantastic notices, quite a few derogatory ones, but we had a hit on our hands.

Graham Greene wrote a letter in *The Times* saying we were the best play in London. Managements fought over who would bring us into town. And my mother loved it!

Drama Examinations

Authors' Note: At the Actors' Theatre School we have found the duologues to be invaluable in giving students an insight into a wider range of classical and modern work. They have proved particularly useful at end-of-term presentations, as each actor has an opportunity to shine in scenes from a collection of plays that are the best of their kind. Duologues are also excellent entertainment for the audience.

Carol Schroder LLAM, PGCE, London Academy of Music and Drama (LAMDA) Examiner, has this to say:

A new selection of duologues suitable for use in schools, colleges and for examinations is always exciting and useful.

For many busy teachers in schools and further education, a book that includes scenes in a variety of styles, encompassing comedy, tragedy, modern and period drama is to be welcomed. For students, there is a wide choice of material that will stimulate and stretch their creative talents. The informative introduction to each scene is commendable.

The LAMDA acting syllabus is used by colleges both in this country and abroad; therefore this collection would be especially helpful where suitable material is not readily available.

The Duologues

HAEMON   CREON
young   middle-aged

Antigone

Sophocles
Translated by Don Taylor

This translation was commissioned by BBC Television. It was first produced in 1986 and directed by Don Taylor.

Sophocles was born probably in the year 495–494 BC. *Antigone* is usually referred to as part of the Theban Trilogy, which was written over a period of 30 years. Although the play completes the trilogy, it is generally considered to have been the first to be produced – *Oedipus the King* and *Oedipus at Colonus* being the later plays.

In this play Oedipus has long departed life and his two sons, Eteocles and Polynices have killed each other on the battlefield. Eteocles has been buried with full honours as befits a hero, but KING CREON has decreed that Polynices must not be buried, but left in the open to be devoured by kites and vultures. Anyone found disobeying his orders will incur the death penalty

Polynices' sister, Antigone, is determined that her brother shall have full burial rites and sprinkles earth over his body. She is captured by the guards, brought before CREON and sentenced to death.

Antigone is betrothed to CREON's son, HAEMON and in this scene he comes to plead with his father to see reason and spare Antigone's life. CREON insists that Antigone is an enemy of the State and must die. Let her find herself a husband among the dead.

From *Sophocles Plays* by Don Taylor, published by Methuen World Classics, London

HAEMON Father, the most enviable of a man's gifts
    Is the ability to reason clearly,
    And it's not for me to say you are wrong . . .
    But I can sometimes hear what people whisper
    Behind their hands: and everywhere, I hear sympathy
    Expressed for this unfortunate girl,
    Condemned, as she is, to a horrifying death
    That no woman has ever suffered before,
    And unjustly, in most people's eyes.
    In burying her brother, who was killed
    In action, she did something most people consider
    Decent and honourable – rather than leaving him
    Naked on the battlefield, for the dogs to tear at
    And kites and scavengers to pick to the bone . . .
    Sir, your reputation matters to me
    As much as your good health and happiness do,
    Indeed, your good name matters more.
    What can a loving son be more jealous of
    Than his father's reputation, and what could please
    A father more than to see his son's concern
    That people will think well of him?
    Then let me beg you to have second thoughts,
    And not be certain that your own opinion
    Is the only right one, and that all men share it . . .
CREON . . . Am I expected to listen
    And take lessons in political tactics
    At my age, from a mere boy?
HAEMON I'm a man, Father, and my arguments are just.
    They stand upon their merits, not my age.
CREON Oh, they stand upon their merits do they? What merit
    Is there, please tell me, in breaking the law?
HAEMON If she'd done something shameful I wouldn't defend her.
CREON She has brought the law into contempt! That's shameful!
HAEMON Listen to the people in the street, Father,
    The ordinary Thebans! They say she hasn't!
CREON I have never based my political principles
    On the opinions of people in the street!
HAEMON Now you're the one who's speaking like a boy!
CREON I'm speaking like a king. It's my responsibility,
    And I will act according to my own convictions!
HAEMON When the State becomes one man it ceases to be a State!

CREON The State is the statesman who rules it, it reflects
His judgement, it belongs to him!
HAEMON Go and rule in the desert then! There's nobody there
To argue with you! What a king you'll be there!
CREON This boy of mine is on the woman's side!
HAEMON Yes, if *you* are a woman, I am.
I'm on your side Father, I'm fighting for you.
CREON You damned impertinent devil! Every word
You say is against me. Your own father!
HAEMON When I know you are wrong, I have to speak.
CREON How am I wrong? By maintaining my position
And the authority of the State? Is that wrong?
HAEMON When position and authority
Ride roughshod over moral feeling . . .
CREON You're weak, and uxorious, and contemptible,
With no will of your own. You're a woman's mouthpiece!
HAEMON I'm not ashamed of what I'm saying.
CREON Every word you have said pleads for her cause.
HAEMON I plead for you, and for myself,
And for common humanity, respect for the dead!
CREON You will never marry that woman, she won't
Live long enough to see that day!
HAEMON If she dies,
She won't die alone. There'll be two deaths, not one.
CREON Are you threatening me? How dare you threaten . . .
HAEMON No, that's not a threat. I'm telling you
Your policy was misbegotten from the beginning.
CREON Misbegotten! Dear God, if anything's misbegotten
Here, it's my son. You'll regret this, I promise you.
HAEMON If you weren't my father, I'd say you were demented.
CREON Don't father me! You're a woman's plaything,
A tame lap dog!
HAEMON Is anyone else
Allowed to speak? Must you have the last word
In everything, must all the rest of us be gagged?
CREON I must, and I will! And you, I promise you,
Will regret what you have spoken here
Today. I will not be sneered at or contradicted
By anyone. Sons can be punished too.
Bring her out, the bitch, let her die here and now,
In the open, with her bridegroom beside her

As a witness! You can watch the execution!
HAEMON That's one sight I shall never see!
Nor from this moment, Father, will you
Ever see me again. Those that wish
To stay and watch this disgusting spectacle
In company with a madman, are welcome to it!
Exit Haemon.

ANIL
20s
Indian

RAVI
20s
Indian

Borderline
Hanif Kureishi

First performed at the Royal Court Theatre in 1981.

Susan, a young journalist who has just returned from India, is gathering information for a radio programme about the Asian community in London. On her way back on the coach to London she meets RAVI, a young Indian from a small village outside Jullanda. This is his first visit to England and he is expecting to stay with his friend, ANIL, who has been living in Ealing for some time now. Unknown to RAVI, ANIL has married an English girl, although he already has a wife and children in his village at home.

In this scene RAVI is walking along the street swinging his suitcase. He stops outside ANIL's house, yelling at the top of his voice.

From *Outskirts and Other Plays*, published by Faber & Faber, London

RAVI Anil! Anil – my brother! It's me – Ravi. Which house is it? [*Pause*] Anil! I've arrived in beautiful England. Did you get my letter?

ANIL [*Opening a window*] What's that noise? Are you insane?

RAVI Anil, you bloody bastard, my only spiritual brother. It's your best friend!

ANIL I've got no friends. [*He makes to go inside*]

RAVI Wait! Don't you recognize me? It's Ravi.

ANIL It's Ravi. Oh, fuck.

RAVI Yes. Ravi. We played in the fields together as children, Anil. Our arses were wiped by your cousin's relations. We had our thread ceremony on the same day. Now I've come across the world to stay with you.

ANIL But what for?

RAVI Oh welcome me to beautiful England, Anil.

18

ANIL [*Under his breath*] Oh, fuck.

RAVI What?

ANIL Welcome . . .

RAVI Anil, it's taken me two days to find you. Why didn't you tell your wife you changed address. You don't realise what a relief it is to see your happy face.

ANIL And you don't realise what a small room I have.

RAVI I'm coming up.

ANIL No, no, no, no, wait, no. [*Anil emerges. They embrace*] Ravi, how did you afford to come here?

RAVI Let's go in first.

ANIL Wait. Tell me how you came.

RAVI My father sold the land.

ANIL What? Fertile land?

RAVI Every worm in it, every animal on it.

ANIL That's typical of your bone-headed father, if I may say so.

RAVI And the farming equipment, the sheds, the plough. He said I'd soon make it up in England.

ANIL What? Ravi, you've been badly misinformed, misled and given entirely wrong information by your rotten relations. England's a cemetery.

RAVI Is it?

ANIL A crematorium.

RAVI Anil, but everyone returns to the village rich from England. I've seen it with these eyes.

ANIL Not any more.

RAVI I'm tired Anil. I want to lie down. I'm hungry. Let's eat together.

ANIL Wait. How I like the air in Ealing, It has a calming effect on my soul.

RAVI Listen. I heard your uncle talking in the village before I left. He was in England once. There was an English girl.

ANIL Which English girl?

RAVI He met, he met. She said; 'Are you Indian?' he said, 'Yes, are you English?' She said 'Yes, I'm English.' He said 'You're English are you? Then undress!'

ANIL It's nothing like that here.

RAVI No, not at first.

ANIL Not at all, I assure you my brother. Not at all . . . You've got to get used to English ways, Ravi.

RAVI Yes, I want to.

ANIL They're very particular about us integrating.

RAVI Are you integrating, Anil?

ANIL I'm beginning to . . .

RAVI By the way, your wife's looking forward to coming here. She says send the ticket for her and the children as soon as you can. She's been crying, Anil, I know . . .

ANIL Listen, you bastard, I'll break your neck and crush your toes and write to your relatives if you mention my wife in front of my social worker.

RAVI Social worker?

ANIL Yes. We all have them here. To teach us English.

RAVI Really? What a marvellous place England is. I knew it would be.

ANIL Yes.

RAVI But will I get a social worker?

ANIL You? No. Well . . . No . . .

RAVI Anil, if it's going to be too much trouble –

ANIL [*Hopefully*] What trouble, Ravi?

RAVI I can always sleep on the floor.

ANIL [*Sarcastically*] Oh, Ravi, no, no, no.

RAVI I'm so tired I don't mind.

ANIL Oh no, no, no, no, no . . . Go upstairs, Ravi . . .

RAVI I knew I'd be welcomed.

[*Ravi goes in*]

OTTO
30–40s

LEO
30–40s

Design for Living
Noel Coward

First performed on Broadway in 1933 and at the Theatre Royal, Haymarket in 1939, it is described as 'a curious, untypical, amoral and yet oddly touching play, with underlying themes of bisexuality and homosexuality'.

Gilda, OTTO and LEO are three people who, contrary to popular belief, can only survive as a trio. The play opens in a Paris studio where Gilda is living with OTTO. When LEO arrives unexpectedly from London – while OTTO is away on business – Gilda decides to go back with him. For the next 18 months OTTO and Gilda live happily together in their London apartment, although they both admit there is something missing from their lives . . . Then, predictably, OTTO comes back from Paris and the situation changes yet again.

Gilda has decided to leave both men and has crept out of the apartment while they are asleep.

In this scene OTTO is congratulating himself on getting Gilda back again and even commiserating with his old friend, when LEO finds two envelopes addressed to each of them propped up against the brandy bottle on the desk.

From *Coward: Plays Three*, published by Methuen, London

LEO [*very quietly*] Otto.
OTTO What is it?
LEO Look.
Otto comes over to the desk, and they both stand staring at the letters.
OTTO Gilda!
LEO Of course.
OTTO She's gone! She's escaped!

LEO Funny word to use, 'escaped'.

OTTO That's what she's done, all the same, escaped.

LEO The joke is becoming richer.

OTTO Escaped from both of us.

LEO We'd better open them, I suppose.

OTTO [*slowly*] Yes – yes, I suppose we had.

They both open the letters, in silence, and read them.

LEO [*after a pause*] What does yours say?

OTTO [*reading*] 'Good-bye, my clever little dear! Thank you for the keys of the city.'

LEO That's what mine says.

OTTO I wonder where she's gone?

LEO I don't see that that matters much.

OTTO One up to Gilda!

LEO What does she mean, 'Keys of the city'?

OTTO A lot of things.

LEO I feel rather sick.

OTTO Have some sherry?

LEO That's brandy.

OTTO Better still.

He pours out a glass and hands it to Leo.

LEO [*quietly*] Thank you.

OTTO [*pouring one out for himself*] I feel a little sick, too.

LEO Do you think she'll come back?

OTTO No.

LEO She will – she must – she must come back!

OTTO She won't. Not for a long time.

LEO [*drinking his brandy*] It's all my fault, really.

OTTO [*drinking his*] Is it?

LEO Yes. I've, unfortunately, turned out to be successful. Gilda doesn't care for successful people.

OTTO I wonder how much we've lost, with the years?

LEO A lot. I think, practically everything now.

OTTO [*thoughtfully*] Love among the artists. Very difficult, too difficult.

LEO Do you think we could find her?

OTTO No.

LEO We could try.

OTTO Do you want to?

LEO Of course.

OTTO Why? What would be the use?

LEO She might explain a little – a little more clearly.

OTTO What good would that do? We know why she's gone perfectly well.

LEO Because she doesn't want us any more.

OTTO Because she thinks she doesn't want us any more.

LEO I suppose that's as good a reason as any.

OTTO Quite.

LEO All the same, I should like to see her just once – just to find out, really, in so many words –

OTTO [*with sudden fury*] So many words! That's what's wrong with us! So many words – too many words, masses and masses of words, spewed about until we're choked with them. We've argued and probed and dragged our entrails out in front of one another for years! We've explained away the sea and the stars and life and death and our own peace of mind! I'm sick of this endless game of three-handed, spiritual ping-pong – this battling of our little egos in one another's faces! Sick to death of it! Gilda's made a supreme gesture and got out. Good luck to her, I say! Good luck to the old girl – she knows her onions!

Otto refills his glass and drains it at a gulp.

LEO You'll get drunk, swilling down all that brandy on an empty stomach.

OTTO Why not? What else is there to do? Here, have some more as well.

He refills Leo's glass and hands it to him.

LEO All right! Here goes. [*He drains his glass*] Now we start fair.

He refills both their glasses.

OTTO [*raising his glass*] Gilda! [*He drains it*]

LEO [*doing the same*] Gilda! [*He drains it*]

OTTO That's better, isn't it? Much, much better.

LEO Excellent. We shall be sick as dogs!

OTTO Good for our livers.

LEO Good for our immortal souls. [*He refills the glasses, and raises his*] Our Immortal Souls!

OTTO [*raising his*] Our Immortal Souls!

They both drain them to the last drop.

JACK
young

ALGERNON
young

The Importance of Being Earnest
Oscar Wilde

This comedy of manners was first performed at St James's Theatre, London in 1895.

JACK WORTHING, under the assumed name of 'Ernest', has declared his love for the Honourable Gwendolen Fairfax. However, when he tries to convince her mother, 'Lady Bracknell' of his suitability as a husband, she questions him about his family and he has to confess that he has lost both his parents and was, in fact, found in a handbag at Victoria Station – the Brighton Line.

As Lady Bracknell sweeps out of the room in majestic indignation, JACK's friend, ALGERNON can be heard outside playing 'The Wedding March'. JACK is perfectly furious. He flings open the door and shouts to ALGERNON to stop playing.

Published by *New Mermaids*, A & C Black, London

JACK For goodness' sake don't play that ghastly tune, Algy! How idiotic you are!
The music stops and Algernon enters cheerily.
ALGERNON Didn't it go off all right, old boy? You don't mean to say Gwendolen refused you? I know it is a way she has. She is always refusing people. I think it is most ill-natured of her.
JACK Oh, Gwendolen is as right as a trivet. As far as she is concerned, we are engaged. Her mother is perfectly unbearable. Never met such a Gorgon . . . I don't really know what a Gorgon is like, but I am quite sure that Lady Bracknell is one. In any case, she is a monster, without being a myth, which is rather unfair . . . I beg your pardon, Algy, I suppose I shouldn't talk about your own aunt in that way before you.
ALGERNON My dear boy, I love hearing my relations abused. It is the only thing that makes me put up with them at all. Relations are

simply a tedious pack of people, who haven't got the remotest knowledge of how to live, nor the smallest instinct about when to die.

JACK Ah! I haven't got any relations. Don't know anything about relations.

ALGERNON You are a lucky fellow. Relations never lend one any money, and won't give one credit, even for genius. They are a sort of aggravated form of the public.

JACK And after all, what does it matter whether a man ever had a father and mother or not? Mothers, of course, are all right. They pay a chap's bills and don't bother him. But fathers bother a chap and never pay his bills. I don't know a single chap at the club who speaks to his father.

ALGERNON Yes! Fathers are certainly not popular just at present. [*Takes up the evening newspaper*]

JACK Popular! I bet you anything you like that there is not a single chap, of all the chaps that you and I know, who would be seen walking down St. James' Street with his own father. [*A pause*] Anything in the papers?

ALGERNON [*still reading*] Nothing.

JACK What a comfort.

ALGERNON There is never anything in the papers, as far as I can see.

JACK I think there is usually a great deal too much in them. They are always bothering one about people one doesn't know, one has never met, and one doesn't care twopence about. Brutes!

ALGERNON I think people one hasn't met are charming. I'm very much interested at present in a girl I have never met; very much interested indeed.

JACK Oh, that is nonsense!

ALGERNON It isn't!

JACK Well, I won't argue about the matter. You always want to argue about things.

ALGERNON That is exactly what things were originally made for.

JACK Upon my word, if I thought that, I'd shoot myself . . . [*A pause*] You don't think there is any chance of Gwendolen becoming like her mother in about a hundred and fifty years, do you, Algy?

ALGERNON All women become like their mothers. That is their tragedy. No man does. That's his.

JACK Is that clever?

ALGERNON It is perfectly phrased! And quite as true as any observation in civilised life should be.

JACK I am sick to death of cleverness. Everybody is clever nowadays. You can't go anywhere without meeting clever people. The thing has become an absolute public nuisance. I wish to goodness we had a few fools left.

ALGERNON We have.

JACK I should extremely like to meet them. What do they talk about?

ALGERNON The fools? Oh! about the clever people of course.

JACK What fools.

ALGERNON By the way, did you tell Gwendolen the truth about your being Ernest in town, and Jack in the country?

JACK [*in a very patronising manner*] My dear fellow, the truth isn't quite the sort of thing one tells to a nice, sweet, refined girl. What extraordinary ideas you have about the way to behave to a woman!

ALGERNON The only way to behave to a woman is to make love to her, if she is pretty, and to some one else, if she is plain.

JACK Oh, that is nonsense.

ALGERNON What about the young lady whose guardian you are! Miss Cardew? What about your brother? What about the profligate Ernest?

JACK Oh! Cecily is all right. Before the end of the week I shall have got rid of my brother . . . I think I'll probably kill him in Paris.

ALGERNON Why Paris?

JACK Oh! Less trouble: no nonsense about a funeral and that sort of thing – yes, I'll kill him in Paris . . . Apoplexy will do perfectly well. Lots of people die of apoplexy, quite suddenly, don't they?

ALGERNON Yes, but it's hereditary, my dear fellow. It's a sort of thing that runs in families.

JACK Good heavens! Then I certainly won't choose that. What can I say?

ALGERNON Oh! Say influenza.

JACK Oh, no! that wouldn't sound probable at all. Far too many people have had it.

ALGERNON Oh well! Say anything you choose. Say a severe chill. That's all right.

JACK You are sure a severe chill isn't hereditary, or anything dreadful of that kind?

ALGERNON Of course it isn't.

JACK Very well then. That is settled.

ALGERNON But I thought you said that . . . Miss Cardew was a little too much interested in your poor brother Ernest? Won't she feel his loss a good deal?

JACK Oh! that is all right. Cecily is not a silly romantic girl, I am glad to say. She has got a capital appetite, goes long walks, and pays no attention at all to her lessons.

ALGERNON I would rather like to see Cecily.

JACK I will take very good care you never do. And you are not to speak of her as Cecily.

ALGERNON Ah! I believe she is plain. Yes: I know perfectly well what she is like. She is one of those dull, intellectual girls one meets all over the place. Girls who have got large minds and large feet. I am sure she is more than usually plain, and I expect she is about thirty-nine, and looks it.

JACK She happens to be excessively pretty, and she is only just eighteen.

ALGERNON Have you told Gwendolen yet that you have an excessively pretty ward who is only just eighteen?

JACK Oh! one doesn't blurt these things out to people. Life is a question of tact. One leads up to the thing gradually. Cecily and Gwendolen are perfectly certain to be extremely great friends. I'll bet you anything you like that half an hour after they have met, they will be calling each other sister.

ALGERNON Women only do that when they have called each other a lot of other things first. Now, my dear boy, if we want to get a good table at Willis's, we really must go and dress. Do you know it is nearly seven?

JACK [*irritably*] Oh! it always is nearly seven.

ALGERNON Well, I'm hungry.

JACK I never knew you when you weren't . . . However, all right. I'll go round to the Albany and meet you at Willis's at eight. You can call for me on your way, if you like.

ALGERNON What shall we do after dinner? Go to a theatre?

JACK Oh, no! I loathe listening.

ALGERNON Well, let us go to the Club?

JACK Oh, no! I hate talking.

ALGERNON Well, we might trot round to the Empire at ten?

JACK Oh, no! I can't bear looking at things. It is so silly.

ALGERNON Well, what shall we do?

JACK Nothing!

ALGERNON It is awfully hard work doing nothing. However, I don't mind hard work where there is no definite object of any kind . . .

BILLY   PC BUTTS
32   young/middle-aged

The Jollies
Alan Ayckbourn

This family play was first performed at the Stephen Joseph Theatre, Scarborough in December, 2002.

It is BILLY's seventh birthday and as a special treat, his mother 'Jilly' takes him and his older sister, Polly, to see the Great Magico at their local theatre.

Young BILLY insists on attending the performance wearing his plastic knight's helmet and carrying a small plastic sword. At first he seems to take no notice of the Great Magico, but when the mysterious cabinet of Shadan, High Priestess of the Mountain Air is wheeled on and the Magician's Assistant asks for volunteers, BILLY rushes up onto the stage. He is led into the cabinet and the curtains are drawn, but when they open again BILLY has vanished – and doesn't come back again. Finally a fully grown man emerges, wearing Billy's plastic helmet and carrying the plastic sword. He insists that he is BILLY and goes back and sits down next to his mother. 'Jilly' leaps up onto the stage and before the Great Magico can stop her, runs into the cabinet, calling out for BILLY . . . And reappears as an eight-year-old girl. The audience is in uproar and the police are called.

In this scene PC BUTTS attempts to interview BILLY.

Published by Faber & Faber, London

PC BUTTS I understand someone's registered a complaint. Is that correct? . . . [*to Billy*] Is that correct, sir? Are you the person who's registered a complaint alleging malpractice from a professional prestidigitator, sir?
BILLY [*startled*] What?
PC BUTTS . . . Now then. What seems to be the problem?

BILLY [*solemnly*] It's my birthday today.

PC BUTTS [startled] Is it?

BILLY I got this sword for my birthday. And this helmet.

PC BUTTS Did you, now?

BILLY I got a whole suit of armour, too. Only my mum wouldn't let me wear it, not to the theatre, 'cos it wouldn't fit under my coat.

PC BUTTS Ah.

BILLY And I got some sweets from my sister Polly only they were ginger and I don't like ginger sweets very much, really. Do you like ginger?

PC BUTTS Er – well, I can take it or leave it, sir, I – Listen, could we –

BILLY My sister likes ginger. That's why she bought me ginger because she likes ginger . . .

PC BUTTS Well, that's –

BILLY And my dad sent me a proper pen. It's a really good one with real ink. He doesn't live with us any more because my mum wouldn't let him because he was adulterating with Mrs Washburn in his office.

PC BUTTS I don't feel that's altogether appropriate, sir, is it? Your domestic arrangements are hardly germane . . .

BILLY Do you have a sister?

PC BUTTS No, I don't. I have two brothers, if you must know.

BILLY I wish I had a brother. Is your brother bigger than you?

PC BUTTS – er, well, one of them is.

BILLY I hate my sister. I would like to push her out of the window and drown her.

PC BUTTS [*laughing nervously*] Well, I'm sure we all feel a little like that occasionally, don't we?

BILLY I would like to cut off her hair and poison her with the fly-spray –

PC BUTTS Now, I think we ought to be –

BILLY I'd like to put poison spiders in her bed and snakes in her bath . . .

PC BUTTS Yes, I think that's quite enough, now, sir . . .

BILLY And put worms in her dinner so that she eats them all up . . .

PC BUTTS [*alarmed now, calling off*] Girls!

BILLY I would put earwigs in her pillow . . . and they would come and nibble her ears . . .

PC BUTTS Would you like to come back over here a moment, please . . .

BILLY . . . I would put t'rantulas in her shoes . . .

PC BUTTS Quick as you can, girls . . . Listen, I – think your dad may be having a bit of a turn. Is your mum with you? Because I think you ought to be getting him home fairly soon . . .

Billy is now fighting off imaginary adversaries with his sword.

BILLY [*as he fights*] . . . kill her with the sword – with the sword . . . [*Exiting*]

DAVID GARRICK   SAM CAUTHERLEY
30s   young man

A Laughing Matter
April De Angelis

First produced by Out of Joint and the Royal National Theatre at the
Yvonne Arnaud Theatre, Guildford in October 2002. The play
transferred to the National in November in repertoire with Oliver
Goldsmith's *She Stoops to Conquer* and returned there in February
2003.

Set in 18th century London, it is described as 'an irreverent version
of real-life events'. It tells the story of David Garrick, Dr Johnson,
Oliver Goldsmith and a new play, *She Stoops to Conquer*, written by
Goldsmith. Caught up between financial pressures and artistic
ambition, GARRICK must make up his mind whether to risk staging
a play which could make or break his career.

SAM CAUTHERLEY is a young protégée of GARRICK's – found as a
baby on the steps of the theatre with a note pinned to him reading
'Gentleman'. Now he has completed his schooling and GARRICK is
grooming him to become an actor.

In this scene GARRICK asks CAUTHERLEY how he is finding
theatrical life. He reads out the report on the week's performances
from the ledger and asks what makes him 'fail so miserably'.

Published by Faber & Faber, London

GARRICK So, Mr Cautherley, how are you finding theatrical life?
CAUTHERLEY All right, thank you, Mr Garrick.
GARRICK Drury Lane has to be good tonight, Mr Cautherley. *She
Stoops to Conquer* opens at Covent Garden. We want to take the
laurels.
CAUTHERLEY I don't see how we can, Mr Garrick.
GARRICK Now don't take that attitude. We've no choice in the
matter. We must sell the play to the audience. It must appear as if

31

we relish every word. That way we convince them it's a masterpiece.

CAUTHERLEY But I know you to be a good judge of plays, sir. I don't understand.

GARRICK Let me worry about my judgement. Now, let's see what Mrs Butler has to say about how you've been doing. [*He opens ledger*] Tuesday 8th September. *Macbeth*. Mr Cautherley fit of giggles on seeing beards of witches. Failure to exit. Friday 11th. *Antony and Cleopatra*. Mr Cautherley forgets to bring on asp. Cleopatra suffocates herself with pillow.

CAUTHERLEY I don't think anybody noticed.

GARRICK Saturday 12th. Lines lost. Cautherley makes up bollocks. And so on. Ah, Wednesday 9th. Mr Cautherley rendered inaudible by squeaking. Can you explain that to me?

CAUTHERLEY That wasn't my fault. Macklin let rip the most enormous fart.

GARRICK If it's not in the play, it hasn't happened.

CAUTHERLEY But it did happen and the first ten rows can stand me witness.

GARRICK When I was your age, I walked to London with sixpence in my pocket. I hung around the theatre till they thought I was part of the furniture. I would have died and gone to heaven if I'd had half the opportunities you've had. Now I know you have promise, sir, and I don't like to be proved wrong. So what is it that makes you fail so miserably? Let's start with Charles Millward.

CAUTHERLEY I don't like him, Mr Garrick.

GARRICK What's wrong with him?

CAUTHERLEY He's in love all the time.

GARRICK He's the romantic lead, Mr Cautherley. People want to feel for somebody when they come to the theatre.

CAUTHERLEY Lumpkin. I could have played that part, Mr Garrick. I had a feeling for it.

GARRICK I have made my decision. Trust me. You are better appearing as a young gentleman.

CAUTHERLEY You mean because I do not know my parents.

GARRICK You have become a gentleman, sir, through your character, as I have. That is why I recommend you leave the Lumpkins of this world well alone.

CAUTHERLEY At school, sir, because I was no one they treated me accordingly.

GARRICK Well, that was very bad, sir.

CAUTHERLEY I used to dream of some way to get back at them. Lumpkin does that.

GARRICK I am sorry you were not happy at school, Sam, but I cannot programme my theatre to satisfy a boyhood grudge. You do see that?

CAUTHERLEY I know I am indebted to you.

GARRICK Yes.

CAUTHERLEY I was very grateful to come to you in the holidays, sir. I remember you impersonated a turkey.

GARRICK Did I?

CAUTHERLEY And a drunk, and Mrs Garrick.

GARRICK I still do a very good Mrs Garrick.

CAUTHERLEY I only ever laughed when I was at your house. I remembered what you did and then I did it for the boys at school. I used to pretend I was your son, sir. Perhaps if I was I would not exercise you as I do.

GARRICK We live in a world where we cannot always do as we wish. People think I'll be selling the patent, but I'd like to pass this place on to a friend. I'm looking for that friend all the time, eh, Sam? Charles Millward is just one part. There'll be others you like better. Study hard, my boy, for seven years, and you may play the rest of your life.

CAUTHERLEY Yes, Mr Garrick.

GARRICK So, tonight?

CAUTHERLEY I won't let you down, sir.

GARRICK Good lad.

Cautherley exits.

JAMIE
33
American

EDMUND
23
American

Long Day's Journey into Night
Eugene O'Neill

Written in 1940 and produced at the Royal Dramatic Theatre, Stockholm in 1956 and later that year at the Helen Hayes Theater, New York.

The play is set in the summer of 1912 and is autobiographical, recreating O'Neill's own painful experiences as the youngest son of an Irish American family with a drug-addicted mother, a tight-fisted father and a drunken and degenerate elder brother.

EDMUND is sitting in the living room reading a book. He looks pale and ill. There is a tray with a bottle of bourbon and whisky glasses beside him. His manner is nervous and apprehensive. As he hears his brother JAMIE enter the house he pours himself a quick drink, replaces his glass and returns to reading his book as JAMIE comes into the room. JAMIE has his coat over his arm and has taken off his collar and tie. He wipes the sweat from his forehead, takes one look at the bottle and glasses and smiles cynically.

Published by Jonathan Cape, London

JAMIE Sneaking one, eh? Cut out the bluff, Kid. You're a rottener actor than I am.

EDMUND [*grins*] Yes, I grabbed one while the going was good.

JAMIE [*puts a hand affectionately on his shoulder*] That's better. Why kid me? We're pals, aren't we?

EDMUND I wasn't sure it was you coming.

JAMIE I made the Old Man look at his watch. I was halfway up the walk when Cathleen burst into song. Our wild Irish lark! She ought to be a train announcer.

EDMUND That's what drove me to drink. Why don't you sneak one while you've got a chance?

JAMIE I was thinking of that little thing. [*He goes quickly to the window at right*] The Old Man was talking to old Captain Turner. Yes, he's still at it. [*He comes back and takes a drink*] And now to cover up from his eagle eye. [*He memorises the level in the bottle after every drink. He measures two drinks of water and pours them in the whiskey bottle and shakes it up*] There. That fixes it. [*He pours water in the glass and sets it on the table by Edmund*] And here's the water you've been drinking.

EDMUND Fine! You don't think it will fool him, do you?

JAMIE Maybe not, but he can't prove it. [*Putting on his collar and tie*] I hope he doesn't forget lunch listening to himself talk. I'm hungry. [*He sits across the table from Edmund – irritably*] That's what I hate about working down in front. He puts on an act for every damned fool that comes along.

EDMUND [*gloomily*] You're in luck to be hungry. The way I feel I don't care if I ever eat again.

JAMIE [*gives him a glance of concern*] Listen, Kid. You know me. I've never lectured you, but Doctor Hardy was right when he told you to cut out the redeye.

EDMUND Oh, I'm going to after he hands me the bad news this afternoon. A few before then won't make any difference.

JAMIE [*hesitates – then slowly*] I'm glad you've got your mind prepared for bad news. It won't be such a jolt. [*He catches Edmund staring at him*] I mean, it's a cinch you're really sick, and it would be wrong dope to kid yourself.

EDMUND [*disturbed*] I'm not. I know how rotten I feel, and the fever and chills I get at night are no joke. I think Doctor Hardy's last guess was right. It must be the damned malaria come back on me.

JAMIE Maybe, but don't be too sure.

EDMUND Why? What do you think it is?

JAMIE Hell, how would I know? I'm no Doc. [*Abruptly*] Where's Mama?

EDMUND Upstairs.

JAMES [*looks at him sharply*] When did she go up?

EDMUND Oh, about the time I came down to the hedge, I guess. She said she was going to take a nap.

JAMIE You didn't tell me –

EDMUND [*defensively*] Why should I? What about it? She was tired out. She didn't get much sleep last night.

JAMIE I know she didn't.

[*A pause. The brothers avoid looking at each other*]

EDMUND That damned foghorn kept me awake, too.

[*Another pause*]

JAMIE She's been upstairs alone all morning, eh? You haven't seen her?

EDMUND No. I've been reading here. I wanted to give her a chance to sleep.

JAMIE Is she coming down to lunch?

EDMUND Of course.

JAMIE [*dryly*] No of course about it. She might not want any lunch. Or she might start having most of her meals alone upstairs. That's happened, hasn't it?

EDMUND [*with frightened resentment*] Cut it out, Jamie! Can't you think anything but –? [*Persuasively*] You're all wrong to suspect anything. Cathleen saw her not long ago. Mama didn't tell her she wouldn't be down to lunch.

JAMIE Then she wasn't taking a nap?

EDMUND Not right then, but she was lying down, Cathleen said.

JAMIE In the spare room?

EDMUND Yes. For Pete's sake, what of it?

JAMIE [*bursts out*] You damned fool! Why did you leave her alone so long? Why didn't you stick around?

EDMUND Because she accused me – and you and Papa – of spying on her all the time and not trusting her. She made me feel ashamed. I know how rotten it must be for her. And she promised on her sacred word of honour –

JAMIE [*with a bitter weariness*] You ought to know that doesn't mean anything.

EDMUND It does this time!

JAMIE That's what we thought the other times. [*He leans over the table to give his brother's arm an affectionate grasp*] Listen, Kid, I know you think I'm a cynical bastard, but remember I've seen a lot more of this game than you have. You never knew what was really wrong until you were in prep school. Papa and I kept it from you. But I was wise ten years or more before we had to tell you. I know the game backwards and I've been thinking all morning of the way she acted last night when she thought we were asleep. I haven't been able to think of anything else. And now you tell me she got you to leave her alone upstairs all morning.

EDMUND She didn't! You're crazy!

JAMIE [*placatingly*] All right, Kid. Don't start a battle with me. I hope as much as you do I'm crazy. I've been as happy as hell because I'd really begun to believe that this time – [*He stops – looking through the front parlour toward the hall – lowering his voice, hurriedly*] She's coming downstairs. You win on that. I guess I'm a damned suspicious louse.

[*They grow tense with a hopeful, fearful expectancy. Jamie mutters*] Damn! I wish I'd grabbed another drink.

EDMUND Me, too.

[*He coughs nervously and this brings on a real fit of coughing. Jamie glances at him with worried pity*]

MARK STYLER   DR FARQUHAR
50   50s

Mindgame
Anthony Horowitz

First performed at the Mercury Theatre, Colchester in 1999 and transferred to the Vaudeville Theatre, London in 2000. The action takes place one evening in Dr Farquhar's office, in an experimental hospital for the criminally insane.

MARK STYLER, a paperback crime writer, is anxious to interview Easterman, a notorious serial killer, for the new book he is writing. In this scene he is trying to persuade DR FARQUHAR to let him meet Easterman. FARQUHAR explains that this is against hospital policy and is anxious for him to leave, but STYLER is persistent.

Published by Oberon Books, London

FARQUHAR If you were to meet Easterman . . .
STYLER What?
FARQUHAR You wouldn't be afraid of him?
STYLER Afraid of him?
FARQUHAR Yes.
STYLER Should I be? Is he still dangerous?
FARQUHAR He's unpredictable.
STYLER Unpredictable.
FARQUHAR Which can be very dangerous indeed.
STYLER Well, you'll get some security . . .
FARQUHAR Not at this time of night. Security will have gone home . . .
STYLER Maybe I could meet Easterman in his cell.
FARQUHAR Both of you in his cell?
STYLER Him in his cell. Me outside.
FARQUHAR It's sound-proofed. The walls are two foot thick.
STYLER Oh. [*Pause*] Could you restrain him?

FARQUHAR Restrain him?

STYLER In a strait jacket or something.

FARQUHAR [*Frustrated*] Mr Styler . . .

STYLER What have I said now?

FARQUHAR I thought I'd explained the philosophy of Fairfields to you. But now I wonder if you listened to a single word I said!

STYLER I listened.

FARQUHAR The whole purpose of this institution, the founding principle, was to try to get beyond the terror that has for so many years imprisoned the mentally ill.

STYLER [*Helpless*] But you said he was in a cell . . . that the walls were two foot thick.

FARQUHAR That's his choice. It is Easterman who is hiding from us.

STYLER I don't understand.

FARQUIIAR Well maybe if you put yourself in a strait jacket you'd begin to. In fact that's not such a bad idea. Have you even seen a strait jacket, Mr Styler? Have you ever held one? Have you ever put one on?

STYLER No. Of course not.

FARQUHAR Then it's time you were educated.

STYLER Wait a minute . . .

FARQUHAR Let me show you what I mean [*Farquhar takes out a strait jacket*]

STYLER What's going on here? . . .

FARQUHAR Put this on.

STYLER I'm not sure that I want to.

FARQUHAR Of course you don't want to. If you wanted to, there wouldn't be any point.

STYLER No . . .

FARQUHAR Think of your book.

STYLER It's got nothing to do with my book.

FARQUHAR It's got everything to do with it.

STYLER You really think this will help?

FARQUHAR Put this on or there is no book.

Styler takes the strait jacket. He holds it as if it's an alien object.

STYLER I don't know where to start.

FARQUHAR I'll help you. Your arms go in here. [*Farquhar continues as he puts the strait jacket on Styler*] There you are. The left first, then the right. That's it. You are, if you like, embracing the very nature of madness. What do you think it would tell you about yourself, wearing one of these?

STYLER That you were mad.

FARQUHAR [*Still fitting the jacket*] That you were considered mad – it's not quite the same thing. The man who put it on you might believe that you were, in his opinion, mad. But it might occur to you, it might cross your mind that it was in fact the reverse that was true. You might believe that it was he who was mad and you who were perfectly sane.

STYLER I don't understand the point that you're trying to make.

FARQUHAR The point is, that once you're wearing one of these, it no longer makes any difference. You have abrogated control, or rather, control has been taken away from you. It not only devours you. It defines you. A man wearing a strait jacket can only be one of two things. An unsuccessful escapologist or a madman. There . . .

Farquhar stands back. Styler is in the strait jacket.

FARQUHAR How do you feel?

STYLER Helpless.

FARQUHAR You are. Tell me that you're sane.

STYLER What?

FARQUHAR Tell me you're sane.

STYLER I'm sane.

FARQUHAR I don't believe you.

STYLER Okay. You've proved your point.

FARQUHAR Carpet.

STYLER I'm sorry?

FARQUHAR Carpet. Envelope. Wallpaper. Cigarette. Jelly.

STYLER I don't understand you.

FARQUHAR You think I'm talking nonsense.

STYLER Yes.

FARQUHAR But how do you know it is not I who am talking complete sense and you who are hearing nonsense? The strait jacket puts the weight of the argument on my side.

STYLER [*Struggling*] Yes, yes, yes. I was wrong to suggest using it. Now take it off.

Farquhar moves closer to Styler and speaks gently.

FARQUHAR [*Quoting*] 'He does not think there is
anything the matter with him
because one of the things that is
the matter with him
is that he does not think that there is anything
the matter with him.'*

* Quoted from *Interpersonal Perception* by R. D. Laing (1966)

STYLER There's nothing the matter with me. I'm beginning to wonder if there isn't something the matter with you. From the moment I arrived . . . this whole place.

FARQUHAR [*Suddenly mad*] It's a madhouse!

STYLER Bloody hell!

Farquhar turns to the desk and picks up a scalpel. He advances with it menacingly. We should notice that, like the room, his character is rapidly changing.

FARQUHAR Let's take it one step further.

STYLER What are you doing with that?

FARQUHAR Does it make you nervous?

STYLER Of course it does. What do you think?

FARQUHAR You're afraid.

STYLER Look. Put it down and let me go. Why are you playing these games with me?

FARQUHAR Games? Do you remember what Nurse Plimpton said?

STYLER What?

FARQUHAR [*Cruelly imitating her voice*] 'He'll play with you . . . like the devil. And then he'll break you down. He'll destroy you!'

STYLER She was talking about Easterman.

FARQUHAR [*Holding the scalpel*] Let's play games with this.

STYLER What are you going to do with it?

FARQUHAR Well, since you so obliged me by slipping into that strait jacket, I thought I'd begin by cutting out one of your eyes.

STYLER What?

FARQUHAR Your left eye or your right eye? I could give you the choice.

GERARD   BECKETT
20s   50s
Irish

Murmuring Judges
David Hare

First performed in the Olivier Theatre at the Royal National Theatre, London in 1991 and revived as part of the David Hare Trilogy in 1993. The title of the play is from the legal expression meaning 'to speak ill of the judiciary', which is still an offence in Scotland.

The play centres on a young lawyer's first case and takes us through the criminal justice system – involving the police, the courts and the prisons – a system that is cracking at the seams. GERARD MCKINNON is one of three men sent down for five years for robbery, but there is serious doubt about his degree of involvement in the crime.

It is GERARD's first experience of prison. In this scene, he has just been brought in and is being interviewed by BECKETT in the reception area before being sent to his cell.

Published by Faber & Faber, London

BECKETT Strip off.

GERARD I'm sorry?

BECKETT Empty all your pockets and take off your clothes.

GERARD Here?

BECKETT Don't you know the procedures? Haven't you been in prison before?

GERARD No.

BECKETT Weren't you on remand?

GERARD I was on bail.

BECKETT So is this your first time? . . . Why aren't you emptying your pockets? [*Gerard moves to the desk and empties his pockets on to it. Beckett has a plastic bag, which he puts the stuff in*] Here. Your things will go in this bag.

[*Gerard starts to undress*]

BECKETT Why are you so late?

GERARD They took me to Pentonville. But then it turned out there wasn't any room.

BECKETT There's no room here. But we'll make some. Why is it midnight?

GERARD Then there wasn't a van.

BECKETT Again?

GERARD They couldn't find one.

BECKETT Have you eaten?

GERARD I had some spaghetti. But then I lost it.

BECKETT How are you feeling?

GERARD Not very well.

[*Beckett is filling out forms*]

BECKETT We've put you on D-wing. We shouldn't really. It's for lifers. But it's that or sleeping in the chapel . . . Sign here.

GERARD I can't. You've taken my pen.

[*Beckett looks at him a moment, not sure if Gerard is taking the piss. Gerard signs*]

BECKETT Would you like a cigarette?

GERARD No, thank you.

BECKETT You're meant to have a shower. But the water's off. So you can get dressed.

GERARD I'm sorry?

BECKETT There's clothes over there. [*Gerard goes over and collects his prison clothes*] Gerard McKinnon.

GERARD Yes.

BECKETT I'm giving you a number. All right? A6324. That's what you'll answer to. Do you need to hear it again?

GERARD No, I've got it.

BECKETT The governor will come and see you in the morning. And we'll fix you with a job. Prison isn't just sitting around.

GERARD No . . . No, I know that.

BECKETT You'll see all the departments. There's a reception committee. Probation, medical, educational, the chaplain. They'll advise you on how to survive in the gaol.

GERARD Survive?

BECKETT Just so you don't waste your time. It's up to you. You can make this place work for you. Anyone can. It's not hard. Get educated. Be sensible.

GERARD Yes. [*He stops a moment, hesitating to speak, halfway dressed*] It's silly, you see, I was sent down with two other people. I was expecting they'd be here with me.

BECKETT That's not the policy.

GERARD No. I'm not complaining. I don't like them that much. It's just . . . they're more experienced. So I thought they might sort of see me through.

BECKETT Yeah. [*He is looking hard at Gerard*] Look, I think someone better tell you. Before you get started. You'd better learn. I've seen people go crazy when it's their first time. [*He pauses*] What you have to do is put the past behind you. Do you understand?

[*Gerard frowns a moment, as he dresses*]

You got done. You did wrong. Society's put you in gaol. OK, now don't brood. Work to the future. Work to the moment when you get out.

GERARD Yes, I see.

BECKETT Because you know what's most dangerous?

GERARD No, I don't.

BECKETT The worst is getting bitter. That's the thing. I watch it. That's the thing that messes people up. Do you see? If you get an attitude. If you get an attitude, I tell you, it's worse than catching the clap. [*He suddenly raises his voice across the area, without warning*] An attitude's the clap. Do you understand me?

GERARD What sort of attitude?

BECKETT If you start thinking, they done me wrong, I'm always in the right, I hate this place, I shouldn't be here, and, pardon my French, sod you all, if you think that, then it kills you. You're finished. It burns you up.

GERARD Yes. [*He looks at Beckett nervously*] I'll tell you what worries me.

BECKETT Yes?

GERARD I got a wife.

BECKETT OK.

GERARD She's not my wife actually. But we have two children. One of them has Down's.

BECKETT Yes. Go on.

GERARD Down's syndrome, you see. [*He pauses, emotion about to overwhelm him for a moment*] And I'm not sure how they'll keep their heads above water.

BECKETT Right, well, that's it, that's what I'm saying. There's some people here going to help you with that. There's people with degrees from Oxford University. They're giving up their lives to help you adjust. So you can live with being banged up. [*He gets up now to go and pick up the old clothes which Gerard has discarded on the floor, and to put them in a bag*] It's a long job. It's not always easy. It's not like changing your clothes.

[*Beckett is now standing directly opposite Gerard*]

GERARD Do you have a belt?

BECKETT You're not allowed a belt. You'll kill yourself. Do you want a cup of tea?

GERARD I won't, thank you. [*There's a moment's pause, things oddly formal and polite*] I'd like to sleep.

BECKETT Good. You look good.

GERARD Thank you.

BECKETT Shall we go up?

LLOYD   TIM

Noises Off
Michael Frayn

First presented at the Lyric Theatre, Hammersmith in 1982. The most recent production was at the Piccadilly Theatre, London in 2001.

Noises Off is not one play, but two – a traditional sex farce, *Nothing On* and the backstage farce that develops during *Nothing On*'s final rehearsal and tour. The two farces begin to interlock, as the characters make their exits from *Nothing On* only to find themselves making entrances into the even worse situation going on backstage.

LLOYD is the director of *Nothing On*. He has been having 'a little thing' with Poppy, the assistant stage manager and Brooke, the juvenile girl.

In this scene LLOYD has popped into the theatre to see Brooke. He is confronted by TIM, the company stage manager and tells him not to let anyone know he's there. He hands him a bottle of whisky for Brooke and gives him some money to go out and buy her some flowers. As far as the rest of the company is concerned – and particularly Poppy – he is in Aberystwyth rehearsing *Richard III*.

Published by Methuen, London

[*Lloyd puts his head back round the door*]
LLOYD Has she gone?
TIM Lloyd! I didn't know you were coming today!
[*Lloyd comes in. He is carrying a bottle of whisky*]
LLOYD I wasn't. I haven't.
TIM Anyway, thank God you're here!
LLOYD I'm not. I'm in Aberystwyth. I'm in the middle of rehearsing *Richard III*.

TIM Dotty and Garry . . .

LLOYD I don't want anyone to know I'm in.

TIM No, but Dotty and Garry . . .

LLOYD I just want two hours alone and undisturbed with Brooke in her dressing-room between shows, then I'm on the 7.25 back to Wales. [*Gives Tim the whisky*] This is for Brooke. Put it somewhere safe. Make sure Selsdon doesn't get his hands on it.

TIM Right. They've had some kind of row . . .

LLOYD Good, good. [*Takes money out of his wallet and gives it to Tim*] There's a little flower shop across the road from the stage door. I want you to buy me some very large and expensive-looking flowers.

TIM Right. Now Dotty's locked herself in her dressing-room . . .

LLOYD Don't let Poppy see them. They're not for Poppy.

TIM No. And she won't speak to anyone . . .

LLOYD First house finishes just after five, yes? Second house starts at seven thirty?

TIM Lloyd, that's what I'm trying to tell you – there may not *be* a show!

LLOYD She hasn't walked out already?

TIM No one knows *what* she's doing! She's locked in her dressing-room! She won't speak to anyone!

LLOYD You've called beginners?

TIM Yes!

LLOYD I can't play a complete love scene from cold in five minutes. It's not dramatically possible.

TIM She's had bust-ups with Garry before, of course.

LLOYD Brooke's had a bust-up with Garry?

TIM Brooke? Not Brooke – Dotty!

LLOYD Oh, Dotty.

TIM I mean, they had the famous bust-up the week before last, when we were playing Worksop.

LLOYD Right, right, you told me on the phone.

TIM She went out with this journalist bloke . . .

LLOYD Journalist – yes, yes . . .

TIM But you know Garry threatened to kill him?

LLOYD Killed him, yes, I know. Listen, don't worry about Dotty – she's got money in the show.

TIM Yes, but now it's happened again! Two o'clock this morning I'm woken up by this great banging on my door. It's Garry. Do I know where Dotty is? She hasn't come home.

LLOYD Tim, let me tell you something about *my* life. I have the Duke of Buckingham on the phone to me for an hour after rehearsal every evening complaining that the Duke of Gloucester is sucking boiled sweets through his speeches. The Duke of Clarence is off for the entire week doing a commercial for Madeira. Richard himself – would you believe? – Richard III? [*He demonstrates*] – has now gone down with a back problem. I keep getting messages from Brooke about how unhappy she is here and now she's got herself a doctor's certificate for nervous exhaustion – she's going to walk! I have no time to find or rehearse another Vicki. I have just one afternoon, while Richard is fitted for a surgical corset, to cure Brooke of nervous exhaustion, with no medical aids except a little whisky – you've got the whisky? – a few flowers – you've got the money for the flowers? – and a certain faded charm. So I haven't come to the theatre to hear about other people's problems. I've come to be taken out of myself and preferably not put back again.

TIM Yes, but Lloyd . . .

LLOYD Have you done the front-of-house calls?

TIM Oh, the front-of-house calls!

[*Tim hurries to the microphone in the prompt corner, still holding the money and whisky*]

LLOYD And don't let Poppy see those flowers!

Exit Lloyd through the pass door.

TIM [*into microphone*] Ladies and gentlemen, will you please take your seats. The curtain will rise in three minutes.

AKOGUN
middle-aged
African

OROONOKO
young
African

Oroonoko

Aphra Behn
A new adaptation by 'Biyi Bandele

This new adaptation of Aphra Behn's novella was first performed by the Royal Shakespeare Company at The Other Place, Stratford-upon-Avon in 1999.

It tells the story of a young African Prince, OROONOKO, who is tricked into slavery, separated from his love, the Princess Imoinda, and transported to the British colony of Surinam in South America, where he is persuaded to lead a slave revolt.

This early scene is set in a military camp on the outskirts of the West African Kingdom of Coramantien. OROONOKO is busy re-stringing his bow when his friends Aboan and Laye enter with other young conscripts carrying drums. They run over to OROONOKO, drag him to his feet and insist he plays the game 'Old Sage You Danced' with them. While OROONOKO is carried away with his performance as 'Old Sage', the AKOGUN — Generalissimo and Head of the Kingdom's Armed Forces — appears. The conscripts have already spotted the AKOGUN and quickly retreat, leaving OROONOKO still dancing. The OKOGUN watches him with bemused interest and then barks out his name.

Published by Amber Lane Press, Oxford

AKOGUN [*barks*] Oroonoko!
[*Oroonoko practically jumps out of his skin*]
OROONOKO My Lord!
AKOGUN What exactly do you
    Think you're doing
    Oroonoko?

OROONOKO I . . . we were playing
  'Old Sage You Danced'.
AKOGUN Old-who-you-what?
OROONOKO 'Old Sage You Danced.'
[*The Akogun picks up Oroonoko's broken bow*]
AKOGUN I see. Remind me, Oroonoko,
  What were you meant to be doing
  Out here in the Forest of Demons?
OROONOKO [*gruff with embarrassment*] Training, sir . . .my Lord.
AKOGUN Training to be what?
OROONOKO Warriors, my Lord.
AKOGUN Training to be a warrior,
  That's right. This is a military
  Training ground, not a playground
  For court jesters. Oroonoko.
OROONOKO Yes, my Lord.
  They forced me, my Lord.
  I didn't want to join in, my Lord.
AKOGUN It wasn't your idea. 'They'
  Forced you. You disappoint me,
  Oroonoko. Let me remind you of
  The story of the five fingers –
OROONOKO The five fingers, my Lord?
AKOGUN The first finger said: I'm hungry.
  The second finger said: I'm broke.
  The third finger said: Let's steal some mangoes.
  The fourth finger said: And if the farmer catches us?
  The fifth finger said: Go and steal: I'll stand apart.
  That is the story of the five fingers, Oroonoko.
OROONOKO I'm sure, my Lord.
AKOGUN Each finger had a choice.
  Each finger made a choice.
OROONOKO Yes. my Lord.
AKOGUN Nobody forces you to do a thing.
  Oroonoko. Let me attempt to tell
  You why: His Highness, the King –
OROONOKO – Long may he reign –
AKOGUN – Long may he reign – the King
  Is now getting on in years. In his younger
  Days, he had many sons, thirteen in all.
  Now he has none: they all died in battle.

Conquering when they fell.
I fought alongside those gallant heroes.
I cherish the memory of their bravery.
Now, the King has left for him for his
Successor, one grandchild, son to one
Of these dead victors. This grandchild,
As soon as he could walk, was sent into the
Field to be trained by one of the King's most
Experienced Generals. And from his natural
Inclination to arms, and the occasions of war
Given him, and – we believe, with the good
Conduct of the old General, the boy became,
At the age of seventeen, one of the kingdom's
Most expert captains. Am I getting through
To you, Oroonoko?

OROONOKO Yes, my Lord.

AKOGUN You are a prince, Oroonoko.
The heir apparent to the throne
Of our land, a king-in-waiting.
You have already proved your
Bravery in war, I was there when
You claimed your first scalp, just
As I was when your father,
Abiodun – may he guide you from
The land of the ancestors –
Slew his first man, He was born
A leader, your father, a prince
Among men. And so are you.
Oroonoko. But to be a leader,
It is not enough to excel as a
Warrior. That, and more is required:
To be a leader, you have to lead,
And leadership means taking responsibility.
It was bad enough that you
Took part in that childish game.
That was the least of it. But to try
And evade responsibility . . .

OROONOKO Forgive me, my Lord.

AKOGUN There's nothing to forgive.
But do remember this.
My king-in-the-making:

'I entered but took nothing,'
Will not save the thief.
[*He hands the broken bow back to Oroonoko*]
AKOGUN Hurry up with that bow, warrior.
OROONOKO [*expectantly*] My Lord?
AKOGUN The War Council has decided.
We are going to war.
[*Exit the Akogun*]

SERGEANT KITE

MOB
One of the Mob

The Recruiting Officer
George Farquhar

This Restoration Comedy was first performed at the Theatre Royal, Drury Lane in 1706 and is based on Farquhar's own experience as a recruiting officer in Shrewsbury.

Captain Plume recruits his grenadiers by courting their sweethearts. His sergeant, KITE, even poses as an astrologer in order to persuade the gullible to serve Her Majesty.

In this opening scene SERGEANT KITE enters, accompanied by the sound of a drum, and speaks to the MOB in the Market Square. He singles out 'one of the Mob'*, offering up a cap for him to try on.

*It has been suggested that this character is COSTAIR PEARMAIN, who later appears as one of the new recruits.

The 'cap' – special headwear of grenadier troops; narrow, with a tall, mitre-shaped front

The Mob – lower-class townspeople and countrymen

Published by *New Mermaids*, A & C Black, London

KITE [*Making a speech*] If any gentlemen soldiers, or others, have a mind to serve Her Majesty, and pull down the French king; if any prentices have severe masters, any children have undutiful parents; if any servants have too little wages, or any husband too much wife; let them repair to the noble Sergeant Kite, at the Sign of the Raven, in this good town of Shrewsbury, and they shall receive present relief and entertainment. – Gentlemen, I don't beat my drums here to ensnare or inveigle any man; for you must know,

the Sign of the Raven the Raven Hotel, in Castle Street

gentlemen, that I am a man of honour. Besides, I don't beat up for common soldiers; no, I list only grenadiers, grenadiers, gentlemen – pray, gentlemen, observe this cap – this is the cap of honour, it dubs a man a gentleman in the drawing of a tricker; and he that has the good fortune to be born six foot high was born to be a great man. [*To one of the Mob*] Sir, will you give me leave to try this cap upon your head?

MOB Is there no harm in't? Won't the cap list me?

KITE No, no, no more than I can, – come, let me see how it becomes you.

MOB Are you sure there be no conjuration in it, no gunpowder plot upon me?

KITE No, no, friend; don't fear, man.

MOB My mind misgives me plaguily – let me see it. [*Going to put it on*] It smells woundily of sweat and brimstone; pray, Sergeant, what writing is this upon the face of it?

KITE 'The Crown, or the Bed of Honour'.

MOB Pray now, what may be that same bed of honour?

KITE Oh, a mighty large bed, bigger by half than the great bed of Ware, ten thousand people may lie in't together and never feel one another.

MOB My wife and I would do well to lie in't, for we don't care for feeling one another – but do folk sleep sound in this same bed of honour?

KITE Sound! Aye, so sound that they never wake.

MOB Wauns! I wish again that my wife lay there.

KITE Say you so? Then I find, brother –

MOB Brother! Hold there, friend, I'm no kindred to you that I know of, as yet – look'ee, Sergeant, no coaxing, no wheedling, d'ye see; if I have a mind to list, why so – if not, why 'tis not so – therefore take your cap and your brothership back again, for I an't disposed at this present writing – no coaxing, no brothering me, faith.

KITE I coax! I wheedle! I'm above it. Sir, I have served twenty campaigns. But sir, you talk well, and I must own that you are a man every inch of you, a pretty, young, sprightly fellow – I love a

cap special headwear of grenadier troops, narrow, with a tall, mitre-shaped front

tricker trigger; 'in . . . tricker': instantly

conjuration magic spell

plaguily confoundedly

woundily dreadfully, excessively

the Bed of Honour (death on) the field of battle

fellow with a spirit, but I scorn to coax, 'tis base; though I must say that never in my life have I seen a man better built; how firm and strong he treads, he steps like a castle! But I scorn to wheedle any man – come, honest lad, will you take share of a pot?

MOB Nay, for that matter, I'll spend my penny with the best he that wears a head, that is, begging your pardon, sir, and in a fair way.

KITE Give me your hand then; and now, gentlemen, I have no more to say but this – here's a purse of gold, and there is a tub of humming ale at my quarters; 'tis the Queen's money and the Queen's drink. She's a generous queen and loves her subjects – I hope, gentlemen, you won't refuse the Queen's health?

ALL MOB No, no, no.

KITE Huzza then! Huzza for the Queen, and the honour of Shropshire!

ALL MOB Huzza!

KITE Beat drum.

Exeunt, drummer beating the 'Grenadier March'.

PUSTOBAIKA   KROPILKIN
middle-aged   young man

Summerfolk

Maxim Gorky
A new version by Nick Dear

This version was first performed in the Olivier auditorium of the Royal National Theatre in 1999.

In the early 20th century, Russians of every social class were beginning to sense the onset of a great upheaval. A diverse group of Russians meet, as they do every year, at their summer holiday retreat. Some are frightened at the prospect of change, some are angry and some yearn for a new life.

This scene opens the second act and takes place in front of Bassov the lawyer's dacha at sunset. A clearing surrounded by a dense ring of fir trees. Way back, to one side, is a small open-air stage with benches and various chairs and tables, where a play is to be performed that evening. PUSTOBAIKA, a watchman, is mending a chair as slowly as he can. A whistle is heard offstage and PUSTOBAIKA puts his own whistle to his mouth and answers it. KROPILKIN enters, a rifle over his shoulder, his whistle hanging round his neck.

Note: 'dacha' – a Russian country cottage used especially in summer

Published by Faber & Faber, London

KROPILKIN All right?
PUSTOBAIKA All right?
KROPILKIN [*indicating the direction from which he has come*] Who's got that one this year?
PUSTOBAIKA Suslov. Engineer,
KROPILKIN New people, is it?
PUSTOBAIKA What you mean, new people?

KROPILKIN Not the old people, as had it last year.

Kropilkin lights a cigarette. Pustobaika takes out his pipe. Clearly it's time for a break.

PUSTOBAIKA [*shrugs*] New people. Old people. All the fucking same.

KROPILKIN Townies.

PUSTOBAIKA Yep. Summer folk. Fifteen years I been watchman here. Seen 'em all – lost count. They come and go like pimples on your arse.

KROPILKIN [*laughing*] Pimples, right.

Through the woods pass a group of young people with balalaikas and mandolins. They talk and laugh, and exit.

KROPILKIN Sounds like we're going to have some music!

PUSTOBAIKA [*sourly*] Marvellous.

KROPILKIN [*indicating the stage*] And they're putting on a play, by the look of it.

PUSTOBAIKA Oh, they do that regular. Plenty of leisure time, you understand.

KROPILKIN I never seen a play.

PUSTOBAIKA You ain't missed much.

KROPILKIN You seen one, have you?

PUSTOBAIKA My boy, I've seen dozens, and they're all the fucking same.

KROPILKIN What they like then?

PUSTOBAIKA Nothing complicated about it. First you dress up in clothes that ain't yours. Don't ask why. Next, you mouth off a lot of words, whatever takes your fancy sort of thing. You might be happy, you might be sad: don't matter. You possibly runs up and down a bit – but only on the platform, mind, you don't get off, that's forbidden.

KROPILKIN Why?

PUSTOBAIKA Dunno. It is a bit restrictive. Then you all has a go at each other. Bit of fighting, bit of kissing if you're lucky – just do the first thing as comes into your head, far as I can see.

KROPILKIN And that's it?

Off, a man whistles for his dog, and shouts: 'Bayan! Here boy! Come here! Bayan!' Off, to the other side, we hear a throaty laugh from Dvoetochie.

PUSTOBAIKA Yep. That's acting.

KROPILKIN Well bugger me. I thought it was –

PUSTOBAIKA Well it ain't.

KROPILKIN They sing a song or two, though?

PUSTOBAIKA Not as often as you might expect. The engineer's wife has a go. Sounds like a goose with a belly-ache.

KROPILKIN [*putting out his cigarette*] Here they come.

PUSTOBAIKA [*picking up his tools*] Fine by me.

TOM   REDDINGTON
25   20s
American   American

The Talented Mr Ripley

Phyllis Nagy
Adapted from the novel by Patricia Highsmith

First produced at the Palace Theatre, Watford in 1998 and set in the early 1950s.

TOM RIPLEY is described as 'an utterly compelling, charming and measured psychopath', whose amorality is at the centre of a plot about duplicity and murder. He is sent to Italy to track down Richard Greenleaf, the errant son of a wealthy American couple. His mission takes on a sinister twist as their lives become inextricably entwined and the theatre audience is drawn inside RIPLEY's mind.

This early scene takes place in a 'dive on Mulberry Street'. REDDINGTON enters. He wears a suit. He's nervous and pulls at his tie.

Published by Methuen, London

REDDINGTON I hope I'm not late. Or early. That would be terrible, right?
Reddington sits at a small table. Tom joins him. An adding machine. An impressive, fat, ominous-looking file folder on the floor near Tom. Tom pours out two cups of coffee while Reddington speaks.
REDDINGTON It's easy to forget your income. I mean, the details of income. You know how it is. Irregular jobs. Distractions. Holidays. Dates. Before you know it, you've lost a few fifties. Here and there.
TOM Cream?
REDDINGTON Milk, thanks. So. I was saying. *What* was I saying?
TOM The loss of a few fifties. Here and there.
REDDINGTON Well, yeah. Exactly my point. Cartooning isn't what you might call a regular job providing a regular pay cheque.

TOM Sugar?

REDDINGTON Three, please. So. I was saying. Cartooning. You know. It's an unreliable source of income. Fun. But unreliable.

TOM You ought to watch that. It's dangerous, Mr Reddington.

REDDINGTON What. Comic books?

TOM Sugar. [*takes one precise sip of his coffee*] I'm afraid we're talking about something more significant than a few fifties here and there. According to Internal Revenue records, we're speaking of several thousand dollars of unreported income over the last two years. Three thousand, two hundred and twenty-two dollars and seventy-seven cents. To be precise. After taking certain deductions and exemptions into consideration, that leaves you with tax owing, including late charges, of two hundred dollars and three cents. Which you may now remit via personal cheque made payable to the Internal Revenue Service.

REDDINGTON [*laughs*] Listen, mister. I'm lucky if I made several thousand dollars in the whole of my *life*.

TOM Tax records don't lie. And in your case, there are many, many records. [*Beat*] You're young. Strong. You look strong. There's time.

REDDINGTON Pardon?

TOM There's time. To earn several thousand dollars. [*Beat*] How many dates have you had in the past two years, Mr Reddington? An approximate number will suffice.

REDDINGTON Geez. I didn't know you guys were interested in –

TOM [*interrupts*] We're not. You said something earlier. About losing the details of your income through distractions. Holidays. Dates. So. How many dates? How many holidays?

REDDINGTON What did you say your name was? McMasters? Central office or something?

Tom picks up a business card from the table and holds it up for Reddington to read.

TOM George McAlpin. Manhattan District Internal Revenue Supervisor.

REDDINGTON [*takes the card from Tom, looks it over himself*] Yeah. You did say that. You did. I'm just, well, nothing like this has ever happened to me before and I'm kinda confused so maybe you could slow down and explain the details a little more clearly so –

TOM If you'd prefer, I can refer the matter to my own supervisor, who is responsible for the entire Northeast Sector. He's based on Boston, but should get down to New York sometime next month.

Of course, that would mean your incurring an additional thirty days or . . . [*he punches some numbers into the adding machine*] twelve dollars and twenty-three cents interest and late charges.

Tom takes another sip of his coffee.

REDDINGTON Isn't it a little weird, a tax collector doing business in a dive on Mulberry Street? Most people work in offices.

TOM Most people are terribly unhappy. Most people remain hunched over desks, cubicles rife with other people's germs and never even *dream* they will be contacted by the Internal Revenue Service. [*Beat*] Washington prefers its inspectors to be mobile. No offices, no overhead. We are saving taxpayer dollars, Mr Reddington. You, on the other hand, are so irresponsible as to lose track of your own income. [*Beat*] Have you taken many holidays over the last two years?

REDDINGTON Okay. Listen. I'm just a guy who draws comics. I admit, yeah, maybe I don't pay too much attention at tax time. I give you what I think you're owed. That's all. But I don't want trouble. I don't want visits from supervisors and I certainly don't want anybody poking into my vacation preferences. So. Do I make the cheque payable to you?

TOM Are you attempting to bribe an employee of the Federal Government? Because if you are, Mr Reddington, I shall have to take far more drastic measures. I shall have to report you.

REDDINGTON Hey, hold on just a – Yeah? You're gonna report me? Who you gonna report me to?

TOM To . . . another department.

REDDINGTON Which department? Exactly.

TOM The appropriate department. Would you *like* me to take this further? Would you *like* me to make a telephone call?

REDDINGTON [*backing down*] Please. Mr McAlpin. I wasn't trying to bribe you. I really wasn't. I just –

TOM [*interrupts*] Make your cheque payable to the Internal Revenue Service. Two hundred dollars and three cents.

Reddington writes out a cheque. Tom sips at his coffee. Reddington holds out the cheque to Tom.

TOM Please put the cheque on the table.

Reddington puts the cheque on the table. Tom peers over at it, then picks it up, inspects it, puts it down on the table beside him.

TOM The United States Government thanks you for your custom.

RENTON
young
Edinburgh Scots

SICK BOY
young
Edinburgh Scots

Trainspotting

John Hodge
Adapted from the novel by Irvine Welsh

Filmed on location in Glasgow, Edinburgh and London – a Figment Film made in association with Noel Gay Motion Picture Company Ltd. for Channel Four in 1995.

The story charts the disintegration of a group of friends whose obsession with drugs and mayhem leads them inexorably to self-destruction. MARK RENTON is described as an unrepentant drug abuser, determined to escape all responsibilities of life, despite the help offered to him by his parents.

In this scene he and his friend SICK BOY are making a concerted effort to get off heroin. RENTON describes the downside of coming off the drug to the audience as he joins SICK BOY in the park. SICK BOY has an airgun and is watching out for potential targets through the telescopic sight – children, pensioners, couples, gardeners, etc. – as he talks about his 'unifying theory of life'.

Published by Faber & Faber, London

RENTON The downside of coming off junk was that I knew I would need to mix with my friends again in a state of full consciousness. It was awful: they reminded me so much of myself I could hardly bear to look at them. Take Sick Boy, for instance, he came off junk at the same time as me, not because he wanted to, you understand, but just to annoy me, just to show me how easily he could do it, thereby downgrading my own struggle. Sneaky fucker, don't you think? And when all I wanted to do was lie alone and feel sorry for myself, he insisted on telling me once again about his unifying theory of life.

SICK BOY It's certainly a phenomenon in all walks of life.

RENTON What do you mean?

SICK BOY Well, at one time, you've got it, and then you lose it, and it's gone for ever. All walks of life: George Best, for example, had it and lost it, or David Bowie, or Lou Reed –

RENTON Some of his solo stuff's not bad.

SICK BOY No, it's not bad, but it's not great either, is it? And in your heart you kind of know that although it sounds all right, it's actually just shite.

RENTON So who else?

SICK BOY Charlie Nicholas, David Niven, Malcolm McLaren, Elvis Presley –

RENTON OK, OK, so what's the point you're trying to make?

Sick Boy rests the gun down.

SICK BOY All I'm trying to do is help you understand that *The Name of the Rose* is merely a blip on an otherwise uninterrupted downward trajectory.

RENTON What about *The Untouchables*?

SICK BOY I don't rate that at all.

RENTON Despite the Academy award?

SICK BOY That means fuck all. The sympathy vote.

RENTON Right. So we all get old and then we can't hack it any more. Is that it?

SICK BOY Yeah.

RENTON That's your theory?

SICK BOY Yeah. Beautifully fucking illustrated.

RENTON Give me the gun.

Through the sight again. This time a Skinhead and his muscle-bound dog are in view.

Sick Boy and Renton talk like Sean Connery.

SICK BOY Do you see the beast? Have you got it in your sights?

RENTON Clear enough, Moneypenny. This should present no significant problem.

The gun fires and the dog yelps, jumps up and bites its owner (the Skinhead).

SICK BOY For a vegetarian, Rents, you're a fucking evil shot.

Renton loads up again.

RENTON Without heroin, I attempted to lead a useful and fulfilling life as a good citizen.

Note: Renton's opening speech and final two lines were 'voice-overs' in the original script and we would suggest that they are played to the audience i.e. 'out front'.

ANTIGONE   ISMENE
young   young

Antigone

Sophocles
Translated by Don Taylor

This translation was commissioned by BBC Television. It was first produced in 1986 and directed by Don Taylor.

Sophocles was born probably in the year 495–494 BC, and *Antigone* is usually referred to as part of the Theban Trilogy, which was written over a period of 30 years. Although the play completes the trilogy, it is generally considered to have been the first to be produced – *Oedipus the King* and *Oedipus at Colonus* being the later plays.

Here Oedipus has long since departed life and his two sons, Eteocles and Polynices have killed each other on the battlefield. Eteocles has been buried with full honours as befits a hero, but King Creon has decreed that Polynices must not be buried, but left in the open to be devoured by kites and vultures. Anyone found disobeying his orders will incur the penalty – death by stoning. ANTIGONE is determined that her brother shall be buried with full religious rites, and arranges to meet her sister, ISMENE, to discuss what can be done.

In this scene ANTIGONE and ISMENE meet in secret outside the Palace of Thebes. They are nervous and troubled. ANTIGONE looks round to be sure they cannot be overheard before speaking.

From *Sophocles Plays* by Don Taylor, published by Methuen World Classics, London

ANTIGONE The same blood
  Flows in both our Veins, doesn't it, my sister,
  The blood of Oedipus. And suffering,
  Which was his destiny, is our punishment too,
  The sentence passed on all his children.
  Physical pain, contempt, insults,
  Every kind of dishonour: we've seen them all,
  And endured them all, the two of us.
  But there's more to come. Now, today . . .
  Have you heard it, this new proclamation,
  Which the king has made to the whole city?
  Have you heard how those nearest to us
  Are to be treated, with the contempt
  We reserve for traitors? People we love!
ISMENE No one has told me anything, Antigone,
  I have heard nothing, neither good nor bad
  About anyone we love . . .
ANTIGONE I thought you hadn't. That's why I asked you
  To meet me here, where I can tell you everything
  Without any risk of being overheard.
ISMENE What is it then? More terrible news?
  Something black and frightening, I can see that.
ANTIGONE Well, what do you think, Ismene? Perhaps
  You can guess. We have two brothers,
  Both of them dead. And Creon has decreed
  That a decent burial shall be given to one,
  But not to the other. Eteocles, apparently,
  Has already been buried, with full military honours,
  And all the formalities due to the dead
  Meticulously observed. So that *his* rest
  In the underworld among the heroes is assured.
  But Polynices, who died in agony
  Just as certainly as his brother did,
  Is not to be buried at all. The decree
  Makes that quite plain. *He* is to be left
  Lying where he fell, with no tears,
  And no ceremonies of mourning, to stink
  In the open: till the kites and vultures
  Catch the scent, and tear him to pieces
  And pick him to the bone. Left unburied
  There is no rest for him in the underworld,

No more than here. What a great king
Our Creon is, eh Sister? . . . The punishment
For anyone who disobeys the order
Is public stoning to death. So that's the news,
And you know it now. The time has come
For you too to stand up and be counted
With me: and to show whether you are worthy
Of the honour of being Oedipus' daughter.
ISMENE Wait a minute Antigone, don't be so headstrong!
If all this is as you say it is,
What can I do, one way or the other?
ANTIGONE Just say you will help me. Commit yourself.
ISMENE To do what? Something dangerous?
ANTIGONE Just to give me a hand to lift the body.
It's too heavy for me to move on my own.
ISMENE To bury him you mean? In spite of the decree?
ANTIGONE He is my brother. And like it or not
He's yours too. I won't betray him
Now that he's dead. No one will ever
Throw that in my face.
ISMENE You must be mad!
Creon has publicly forbidden it.
ANTIGONE He can't forbid me to love my brother.
He has neither the right nor the power to do that.
ISMENE Have you forgotten what happened to our father?
Contempt and loathing from everyone,
Even from himself, that was his reward . . .
Think for a moment Antigone, please!
We are women, that's all. Physically weaker –
And barred from any political influence.
How can we fight against the institutionalised strength
Of the male sex? They are in power,
And we have to obey them – this time
And maybe in worse situations than this.
May God forgive me, and the spirits of the dead,
I have no choice! State power
Commands, and I must do as I am told.
When you are powerless, wild gestures
And heroic refusals are reserved for madmen!
ANTIGONE Don't say any more. I won't ask again.
In fact, if you were to offer help now,

I would refuse it. Do as you please.
I intend to bury my brother,
And if I die in the attempt, I shall die
In the knowledge that I have acted justly . . .
Do as you please. Live, by all means.
The laws *you* will break are not of man's making.
ISMENE I reverence them. But how can I defy
The unlimited power of the State? What weapons
Of mine are strong enough for that?
ANTIGONE Fine. That's a good excuse. I'll go
And shovel the earth on my brother's body.
ISMENE I'm frightened, Antigone. I'm frightened for you.
ANTIGONE Don't be frightened for me. Fear for yourself.
ISMENE For God's sake, keep it quiet. Don't tell anyone.
I'll keep our meeting secret.
ANTIGONE Don't you dare!
You must tell everybody, shout it in the streets.
If you keep it secret, I shall begin to hate you.
ISMENE There's a fire burning in you Antigone,
But it makes me go cold just to hear you!
ANTIGONE I'm not doing it to please you. It's for him.
ISMENE This obsession will destroy you! You're certain to fail!
ANTIGONE I shall fail when I have failed. Not before.
ISMENE But you know it's hopeless. Why begin
When you know you can't possibly succeed!
ANTIGONE Be quiet, before I begin to despise you
For talking so feebly! *He* will despise you
Too, and justly. You can go now. Go!
If I'm mad, you can leave me here with my madness
Which will doubtless destroy me soon enough.
Death is the worst thing that can happen,
And some deaths are more honourable than others.
ISMENE If you've made your mind up . . . Antigone, it's
madness . . .
Remember, I love you . . . whatever happens . . .
Exit Antigone and Ismene in opposite directions.

LADY JERSEY
late 30s–40s

CAROLINE
late 20s
German

Battle Royal
Nick Stafford

First performed on the Lyttleton stage of the Royal National Theatre in December 1999.

The play follows the events of the tempestuous marriage of George IV and his outspoken wife, CAROLINE of Brunswick – from their first disastrous meeting in 1795 prior to the wedding, through their inevitable separation and his failed attempt to divorce her for adultery, to her death in 1821.

This scene takes place in the nuptial bedchamber immediately after the wedding. CAROLINE has said goodnight to her maid, Mariette and is joined by LADY JERSEY, Lady of the Bedchamber.

Published by Faber & Faber, London

CAROLINE I thought it went terribly well today.

LADY JERSEY Didn't it? I thought it quite the best wedding I have been to for some time.

CAROLINE Well, it should be, shouldn't it? It should be the best wedding since the last time the heir to the throne was married. Their Majesties have been married thirty-five years, have they not?

LADY JERSEY They have.

CAROLINE Were you a guest?

LADY JERSEY No.

CAROLINE How old were you, then?

LADY JERSEY It must be a great relief to be married at last.

CAROLINE Were you a beauty? I never was. Not pretty-pretty. You must share your secrets with me. The unguents and potions that sustain you. Where is Lord Jersey tonight?

LADY JERSEY He'll still be celebrating your Royal Highness's immense good fortune, I expect.

CAROLINE I understand my husband has appointed your husband Master of Hounds. And here you are, Lady of my Bedchamber. My good fortune gives rise to your good fortune.

LADY JERSEY All of us within the royal compass are indeed blessed.

CAROLINE Tell me about him.

LADY JERSEY About my husband?

CAROLINE My husband. You are his friend.

LADY JERSEY His manners are impeccable. He can illuminate a room if he chooses just by his personality, regardless of his title. He's clever.

CAROLINE Why hasn't he married before?

LADY JERSEY I have no idea.

CAROLINE Why does he marry now?

LADY JERSEY Because it is now that the heir to the throne makes a suitable match.

CAROLINE Tell me his flaws.

LADY JERSEY His flaws?

CAROLINE He had been drinking today. He was completely betrunken. Someone had to hold him up.

LADY JERSEY Your Highness; I don't think it's proper for me to have this conversation with you.

CAROLINE Tell me about his debts.

LADY JERSEY I know nothing of his personal finances.

CAROLINE He likes to spend far too much on finery. This makes some people nervous. They are frightened of comparisons with Louis XV.

LADY JERSEY But the people demand that he live like a prince.

CAROLINE A difficult balance to strike. The times are awful and momentous. The French Revolution. Napoleon. The conduct of all the royal families is closely scrutinised. Radicals and Republicans are constantly alert for any opportunity to foment disunity. I don't want you and I to be enemies.

LADY JERSEY Why should we be enemies?

CAROLINE In Brunswick I received a letter. It warned that you are 'the worst and most dangerous of profligate women', 'driven by envy', intent on my 'ruin'.

LADY JERSEY May I ask who signed this defamation?

CAROLINE It was anonymous.

LADY JERSEY Then I hope your Royal Highness dismissed it as malicious.

CAROLINE But you are hostile towards me. Is it envy? I expect envy from other women despite the fact that my title is one which the overwhelming majority are ineligible to occupy.

Caroline strays near a window. Cheers from a crowd outside.
A servant lowers the lights. The crowd makes ribald noises.
Lady Jersey turns down the bed sheets.

LADY JERSEY You occupy a position of which nearly every woman
dreams, yet none, bar one, can fulfil.

SARAH   MAGGIE
30s–40s   30s–40s
Scots   Scots

Bondagers
Sue Glover

First performed at the Traverse Theatre, Edinburgh in 1991, and set
on a Border farm in 1860.

The bondagers were the women workers of the great Border farms
in the last century. Each farm-worker was hired on condition that he
brought a female worker to work alongside him – if not his wife or
daughter, then some girl that he himself had to hire at the Hiring Fair.

It is a winter evening and the bondagers are waiting anxiously to
see if they are going to be kept on for another season. The 'Maister'
has not spoken to any of them yet. Liza is reading out a letter she has
just received from her brother, Steenie in Canada. He says that work
is plentiful over there and the pay is good. Walter Brotherston – a
young fellow the girls all know and used to work with – now owns
a hundred acres of land.

As Liza goes out musing over her letter, MAGGIE and SARA
remember that 'young limmer' Walter Brotherston.

From *Twentieth Century Scottish Drama* in the Canongate Classics series, published
by Canongate Books, Edinburgh

SARA Walter Brotherston! A hundred acres! [*She starts to laugh*]
    Well, he was a young limmer and no mistake! Remember the night
    of that kirn at Westlea?
MAGGIE [*Frosty*] I certainly do.
SARA [*Enjoying herself*] There were half a dozen bairns – the wee
    ones, just babies – sleeping in the hay at the farthest end of the
    barn. Oh, they were good as gold, not a cheep out of them, and of
    course around dawn everyone started for home, and the mothers
    were tired out, and the babies sleeping like the dead. So it wasn't
    till later, till they were all home, that they found out what Walter
    had done!

MAGGIE He should have been whipped!

SARA It wasn't just him, it was Jamie as well. They'd changed the babies round. They'd changed all the clothes, the bonnets and shawls. Six babies! – and all of them home with the wrong mother!

MAGGIE But they'd notice, the mothers!

SARA [*Laughing*] Eventually! What a squawking and screeching across the fields – it sounded like a fox had got amongst the hens.

MAGGIE [*Muttering under Sara's words*] A swearing scandal, that's what it was!

SARA The blacksmith's bairn was away up the hill with the shepherd and his wife! And Maggie's wee Tam ended up in the village, who was he with again, Maggie, was it Phoebe?

MAGGIE [*Grim*] I went to feed and change my bairn – and he'd turned into a lassie! Oh, you can laugh. But there's many a baby been changed by the Gyptians – so what was I to think? He was never a Christian that Walter Brotherston – and neither's that scoundrel Jamie Dodds. They aye watch him at the kirk! He'll more likely take money out the plate than put anything in.

SARA There's plenty he gives that no one knows of. He gives to the needy. Many a time.

MAGGIE [*Grudgingly*] He's a grand worker. I'll grant you that.

SARA Ay.(. . .) The maister will be keeping *him* on, likely.

[*A pause. These days they are all nagged by the same thought*]

SARA Has he spoken to Andra yet, the maister?

MAGGIE No. Not yet. Has he spoken to you?

SARA No.

ZANDA   BEATRICE
20s   20s
Moroccan

The Clink
Stephen Jeffries

First produced by Paines Plough at the Theatre Royal, Plymouth in
1990 and set in and around 'the Clink' – a prison in Southwark,
London – towards the end of the reign of Elizabeth the First.

ZANDA is a slave shipped over from Morocco and bought by privy
councillor Warburton to look after his daughter, BEATRICE, who is
Lady in Waiting to the Queen. Warburton has arranged for his
daughter to marry Martin Gridling, a man she heartily despises.
ZANDA devises a plot to get rid of him. Gridling is a well-known
'roarer' and the girls disguise themselves as 'roaring girls' and invite
him to a duel. BEATRICE easily wins this duel of words, then takes a
pistol from her cloak and shoots Gridling dead.

In this scene BEATRICE, covered in mud with gunpowder in her
hair, is musing over the murder she has just committed. ZANDA tries
to persuade her to come to bed. They need sleep. The murder must
be concealed at all costs.

Published by Nick Hern Books, London

BEATRICE I see his face. A piece of parchment scratched on by a child
and left out in the rain. The mud of London's fields spattering his
eyes and nose. Mud on my boots. After killing, every action so
loud. I tug at a broken nail, the rip of it deafens me. Again and
again I feel the jolt of the pistol in my hand. The ease of it. The
ecstasy. How now?

ZANDA My lady. Will you come to bed? It is time.

BEATRICE For bed, no, surely. It is night and time to throw on our
roaring apparel and out into the darkness.

ZANDA We will act the perfect maid and lady and follow daily
customs. Your father must harbour no suspicion against us. I will
brush your hair and soothe you, then you'll sleep.

BEATRICE My hair is mud and gunpowder. You will not brush it out, I like it so.

ZANDA Tomorrow we will fetch water to wash it. Now sit.

BEATRICE Who gives the orders here?

ZANDA You are the mistress in the house, but I am Queen in the streets and we have brought the street stink here into your, chambers. You do not know what musks and mists can cover murder but I do and you will swallow my prescription. Now sit.

Beatrice sits on the floor, but not where Zanda has indicated. Zanda goes to her and brushes.

When I was a slave to the Spaniards, I was their thing to use as they wished. I fetched for them, skivvied. They took me, sleeping, in sickness, they didn't care. One was the ship's doctor. He grabbed me, sudden while I slept upon the deck. I turned and fisted him, he fell, heavy, his head striking a cannon. Dead. I held his body up and nailed it to the mast. The crew looked on. They never troubled me again. I said: 'Now I am your doctor.' I had broken the chain.

BEATRICE The chain.

ZANDA As you have broken yours.

BEATRICE And what should I do now?

ZANDA Why, anything, you have freed yourself.

BEATRICE Until the next suitor. Do I kill him too?

ZANDA You wait. You live from day to day. You relish the snapping of your chain.

BEATRICE There is a chain. It links the dumb stones to God. That is what they taught me. For look, the lodestone is above all stones for it seems, in its iron attraction to have some life and so is somewhat of a plant, fibrous, reaching out beyond itself. And some plants of the sea, in their sucking and pulsating imitate the life of creatures. The ape walks upright, the ape apes the man and men, some saintly men are close to angels who fly all the way to God. This is the chain, this is the living chain and I have snapped it.

ZANDA I meant the chain that bound you to your father.

BEATRICE That is not the chain! [*Beatrice stands suddenly. The hairbrush drops to the floor*] I have snapped a link in the chain of being, a small snip to a link and now the chain is sundered, and what is outside the chain? They told me hell, and they told me falsely. I killed but I am not in the furnace. I am in the thrilling region, the realm of ice where the air is dizzy.

ZANDA My lady, I have a soothing plant that you may smoke to calm you –

BEATRICE I have their secret! I know the secret the men have that they carry with them, which gives them power! The swords on their hips, their furtive pistols. Killing is exciting, it is power. You knew that from your slave days and yet you kept it from me.

ZANDA I was in desperate straits.

BEATRICE And so was I, now I am delivered. I am no longer one who waits, looks on and nods agreement. I change the face of the earth. I squeeze a trigger and the world is changed. There is nothing I cannot do!

ZANDA You still have everything to do. You must not trumpet out this murder. Your father will be high in anger at this death and you must play bereavement to the hilt.

BEATRICE I have done with playing. From now I shall play myself at all times.

ZANDA The Queen grows sicker. This is the report from every stair and corridor. When she is dead, your power in the court is gone. All you can ever be is a drain on your father's exchequer or a quim for trading on the market. You have 'scaped one husband, you cannot 'scape them all.

BEATRICE This is not so. I am a killer. I am one of them.

Zanda seizes Beatrice.

ZANDA You and I have been as sisters! We have brought the two halves of the globe together and made a safe cocoon to live in, an egg where we have dwelt in safety from the world of men. The shell is shattered now. We must stand together. Without me you will have no access to the world of pleasure and die a country death with a fat husband. Without you I have no privilege and cannot be protected from the curs who call me blackamoor and spit upon my skin.

BEATRICE And still you do not see it. They put a prayer book in my hand and told me God would see my every sin. But I have done the worst, the final sin and am not seen. I have not put myself in prison, I have burst out. You talk of freedom here on earth, freedom of the body, when I speak of my eternal soul.

ZANDA You must conceal this murder. If you broadcast it abroad, my complicity will be much blamed.

BEATRICE It was a noble thought and you must own it.

ZANDA Speak lower! Your guilt, once known will be laden at my door . . . My Lady Beatrice, you shall go straight to bed –

SISSY   MONA
17   17
American   American

Come Back to the 5 & Dime,
Jimmy Dean, Jimmy Dean
Ed Graczyk

First produced at the Martin Beck Theatre, New York in 1982.

The play is set in a 'Five-and-Dime' in McCarthy – a small town in West Texas. On the walls are framed pictures of James Dean and a crudely painted sign reads, 'The 20th Anniversary Reunion of the Disciples of James Dean September 30th 1955 – September 10th 1975'.

The Disciples of James Dean are gathered together for their 20th reunion. They are now middle-aged women, who were teenagers when James Dean filmed *Giant* two decades ago in nearby Marfa. MONA was an extra on the film and has a child whom she insists was fathered by James Dean and is the 'Jimmy Dean' of the title. The ladies reminisce in flashbacks to their youth: in 1958, SISSY, MONA and their friend Joe, who worked at the Five-and-Dime, formed a lookalike act – *The McGuire Sisters* – for the Senior Talent Show. Local people were shocked and disgusted and Joe was fired from his job.

In this scene young SISSY – wearing a skintight sweater and a short skating skirt – is followed by young MONA; they enter the back room into the store carrying boxes of cosmetics, which they will hang from the display racks.

Published by Samuel French Inc., New York

As flashback to their youth . . .

SISSY [*Entering*] Me an' Joe was gonna get Stella May to take your place doin' the McGuire Sisters, but she wouldn't have been as good as you.

MONA I don't think we should do that act anymore because of all that's happened. Juanita says it was that thing at the senior dance with Lester T. Callahan that started all the trouble.

SISSY I thought it was a riot, a real riot. They all thought he was my cousin from Oklahoma City . . . especially Lester T.

MONA He really does make a very pretty girl, doesn't he?

SISSY Lester T. sure thought so, didn't he? . . . thought he was the cutest thing he'd ever seen. I would have given anythin' to see the expression on his face when he got Joe in the backseat of his car, reached in his dress, squeezed them balloons and strawberry jello exploded all over his rented white tuxedo. [*Laughs*] Serves the bastard right for two-timin' me right in front of my face.

MONA Joe should never have carried the joke so far. You think Lester T. will ever get even with him like he said?

SISSY Shoot, I wouldn't put it past that goon-head.

MONA It's been nearly three months. Maybe he's forgot.

SISSY He ain't forgot . . . hell, it's the only thing outta twelve years of school he's remembered. [*Looks out the window*] Thank God, that rain's finally gonna stop. I got me a date over at the graveyard tonight.

MONA We've got a meetin' of the "Disciples", did you forget?

SISSY The meetin' ain't gonna last all night is it? I just can't get over your bein' back . . . seems like I'm dreamin' or somethin'.

MONA [*Excited*] Oh me too. [*They hug*] I missed you so very much.

SISSY And me, you.

MONA I was so afraid for this summer to be over. Now it can stay summer forever, can't it?

SISSY Shoot, I hope not. The heat's been so hot I think it's beginnin' to shrink my 'bazooms'. [*Throws out her chest*] They look like they've shrunk any to you?

MONA [*Inspecting*] They both look the same to me.

SISSY You think they might be as big as Marilyn Monroe's?

MONA I think they might be bigger.

SISSY [*Thrilled*] You really mean it? Sidney said they were, but you know him.

MONA He told you that?

SISSY He's such a card . . . always pinchin' my bottom behin' one of the counters. Not where Juanita can see him though. She thinks he's as prim an' proper as a preacher. Boy, does he pull the wool over her eyes.

MONA Where is he today, anyhow? . . . hung over again?

SISSY Had some kinda meetin' over in Waco. [*She takes a lipstick, eyebrow pencil, etc. from the rack and applies them*]

MONA I'll never forgive him for firin' Joe.

SISSY Well, whattaya expect from the buttholes in this town?

MONA I'm afraid he might leave town now he's got no job.

SISSY Hey, you got a thing for him maybe?

MONA No!

SISSY You do! That's why you really came back, ain't it?

MONA [*Quickly*] It was my asthma . . . my asthma . . . we're friends, that's all . . . just like you an' me.

SISSY OK . . . OK. Jeez, I was only kiddin' . . . Here try some of this new cheek blush that just come in. [*Starts to apply it on her*] Hey, ain't you just bustin' for that movie to come out so's you can see yourself up there on the movie screen with James Dean? [*A squeal and a shiver*] Ooh! He can drag me off to the graveyard any ol' night he wants . . . rainin' or not.

MONA [*Nervous*] Did you ever dream about what it would be like? You know, to make love to somebody real famous like him?

SISSY All the time . . . but you really should experiment with some 'nobody' before you tackle someone as important as him. That's all I'm doin' . . . sort of like homework for the big test later on. I just can't get over somebody your age haven' never been over to the graveyard with anyone before.

MONA It's . . . it's too spooky.

SISSY Oh, you get used to it after awhile. Some of the guys get scared an' have trouble gettin' goin', but they're mainly after my 'bazooms' anyhow. They all gotta squeeze an' feel aroun' . . . most of 'em get their kicks just doin' that.

MONA Aren't you afraid you'll get caught?

SISSY Shoot, nobody goes over to that ol' graveyard no more. It's all grown over with stickers an' tall grass, an' the gravestones have all been pushed over to use for layin' places. I always do it on top of Colonel Jaspar P. Ramslan' the second . . . soun's dreamy, don't he?

Damsels in Distress: GamePlan

Alan Ayckbourn

First performed at the Stephen Joseph Theatre, Scarborough in May 2001 and at the Duchess Theatre, London in 2002. *GamePlan* is part of a trilogy under the heading, *Damsels in Distress*.

When Lynette's business collapses and her husband disappears, she finds herself a single parent with a dwindling lifestyle. However, her daughter, SORREL has a plan to save them both.

In this scene SORREL outlines her 'game plan' to her friend, KELLY. She has taken advice from another friend, Angie, who advertises on the Internet and is doing very well indeed. KELLY is not too happy about this – especially as SORREL is expecting her to act as her 'Maid'.

Published by Faber & Faber, London

KELLY Please, Sorrel. There must be something else you can do. Not this.

SORREL What else? I've no qualifications, have I? Not yet.

KELLY What about a newspaper round or something?

SORREL Great! Can you see me earning the sort of money we need from a newspaper round?

KELLY There must be something else.

SORREL Kelly, the sort of money I can earn doing this – it's massive. You should see Angie's flat. She's rolling in it. She says it's money for old rope. It really is.

KELLY But don't you have to – you know – do peculiar things to them? The men. If they ask you?

SORREL [*knowledgeably*] No. Not if you don't want to. Depends what line you go into, of course. I mean, Angie, she's a dominatrix. I'd be straight vanilla, of course.

KELLY Be what?

SORREL Vanilla. That's what they call straight sex. Vanilla. As opposed to, say, S & M or BDSM or Animal Training or Water Sports or Adults Babies, say.

KELLY How do you know all this?

SORREL Get on the Internet, Kell. Your eyes will be opened, girl.

KELLY I can't open anything on my machine. I've still got Net Nanny on mine.

SORREL Oh, come on. You bypass that, don't you?

KELLY I can't.

SORREL God, Kell. No wonder you're still a virgin. Honestly.

Pause

KELLY So you're seriously going to go ahead with this?

SORREL Yes.

KELLY Where?

SORREL Here.

KELLY In this flat? What about your mum?

SORREL She's at work from six a.m. till six p.m.

KELLY What about the evenings?

SORREL I'll operate daytimes. You can do it in the daytime as well, Kelly. It is allowed.

KELLY What about school?

SORREL I wouldn't do it every day. Then there's the holidays. Plenty of time, then.

KELLY You've really thought it through, haven't you? How are you going to – I mean, you know, get people?

SORREL Clients?

KELLY You're not going to just walk up and down outside, are you?

SORREL For God's sake, Kelly. Internet. Advertise there. Angie showed me one or two reputable sites. All you give is a phone number.

KELLY This phone number? But what if – ?

SORREL A separate phone number, Kelly. On a mobile. Not even my own mobile. A separate mobile. Business calls only. Miracle of modern technology.

KELLY [*Staring at her*] I just don't know what to say. I don't. I thought I knew you. You're my friend. I don't know you at all. Not at all.

SORREL [*Smiling*] Well. Urgent needs – desperate measures.

KELLY [*A thought dawning*] And what do you want me to do? Cover for you at school? [*Pause*] You don't want me to – I mean you're not planning on – you know, with three of us, are you?

SORREL I wouldn't ask you to do that, Kell. No, I need you to be my maid.

KELLY [*Blankly*] Your maid?

SORREL Angie said I should have one. Particularly when I'm starting out. Just in case of – you know, difficulties.

KELLY Difficulties? What difficulties?

SORREL Someone who can open the door and offer them a drink while they're waiting and yell for help if need be . . .

KELLY [*In panic*] I can't do that. If my mum found out she'd go crazy . . .

Kelly sits miserably. She starts to cry a little.

SORREL Don't start that. Kelly!

KELLY [*Through her tears*] I can't be a maid. I've got nothing to wear. What am I going to wear?

SORREL Well, we'll have to go shopping, won't we? Come on, you love shopping up West. There's several shops.

KELLY What, you mean those – weird shops?

SORREL No. Just underwear and things. And – other items. I may have to borrow a little bit from you, Kell.

KELLY What other items?

SORREL You know. Condoms. We'll need condoms. Masses of those.

KELLY I'm not buying condoms.

SORREL Kelly!

KELLY What if a friend of my parents sees me?

SORREL What would a friend of your parents be doing in a sex shop?

KELLY No, true. They're all a bit past that.

SORREL Precisely. So. Are you game?

LULAMA   ZANDILE
30s   young

Have You Seen Zandile?

Gcina Mhlophe, Maralin Vanrenen and Thembi Mtshali

First performed at the Market theatre, Johannesburg in 1986 and also as part of the Edinburgh Festival at the Traverse Theatre in 1987. It is set in the 60s and is based on Gcina Mhlophe's own life.

ZANDILE lives with her grandmother in Durban. She is a bright child who dreams of growing up to become a teacher – until her world is turned upside-down when she is captured by her natural mother, LULAMA, and expected to conform to the ways of life in the harsh, rural Transkei homeland.

In this scene ZANDILE is working in the field, cutting grass with a sickle for the thatch roof. Her back is sore from bending. LULAMA comes to tell her to hurry up; it is getting late and there is more grass to be cut. She sees the 'letter' ZANDILE was writing to her grandmother and rubs it out with her feet.

Published by Methuen, London

LULAMA Uphi Zandile? Where are you? What are you doing? It's getting late and you must still cut more grass.
ZANDILE Hawu Mama, I'm afraid of the mice.
LULAMA What are they going to do? Are they going to eat you up? [*Sees the letter*] And what is this . . . this child is full of dreams. [*She rubs the letter out with her feet. Zandile and Lulama mime cutting grass with sickles. Lulama looks up at Zandile*] Zandile bend lower. You must cut the grass at the bottom.
ZANDILE The grass is cutting my hands Mama.
LULAMA I don't know what to do with this child now.
ZANDILE And you don't know what to do with me.
LULAMA I want you to grow up and be a strong woman and . . .
ZANDILE I'm going to be a teacher.

LULAMA Not here. You have to work outside here, where the men can see you.

ZANDILE Men can still see me if I teach.

LULAMA Where are you going to teach here? Are you going to teach the goats? Sit down. I want to talk to you. What are you doing?

ZANDILE [*Mumbles, scratching her left leg*] The grass is itchy Mama.

LULAMA . . . In a few years you have to be married. Who do you think you are going to marry if you can't do a woman's work?

ZANDILE I'm not going to get married. I am very good at school.

LULAMA . . . Zandile, listen to me. I was talking to Matshezi the other day. Do you know her son?

ZANDILE Yebo Mama.

LULAMA His family wants you.

ZANDILE But I don't want him.

LULAMA What do you mean you don't want him? His uncle has the richest family in this village. He could have any girl in the village and he chose you. That's how I got married as well. You must have your own house.

ZANDILE But I don't like him. He's got all these ugly scars on his face.

LULAMA But that's our tradition . . . Life is different here. No time for rest – just work. If you learn that then you will make a good wife for Matshezi's son.

ZANDILE I don't know why you took me from Gogo, if you are just going to give me away to Matshezi's son.

LULAMA Zandile I took you because you are my child.

ZANDILE But you don't even let me visit my grandmother.

LULAMA I can't because if I let you go there, you will never come back again. I know you were happy there, I saw you that night.

ZANDILE You saw me Mama?

LULAMA Yes, when I went to visit your grandmother in Durban. [*Sits*] I wanted to take you then, but I knew Gogo would never let you go, after all those years you had become her child.

ZANDILE But you shouldn't have stolen me.

LULAMA How else was I going to get you? Wait till you have a child, you'll know what I've been going through all the years. How do you think it feels, to know that your child doesn't even know you exist?

ZANDILE . . . Why are you in such a hurry to give me away, if you missed me so much?

LULAMA But it's our tradition. It was the same when I got married. By the time I was 22, I already had four children.

ZANDILE But I don't even like him.

LULAMA You don't have to like him, he has to like you. Do you think I was happy with my husband? But he chose me. I had to stay married to him.

ZANDILE But he left you.

LULAMA It's easy for men to go.

ZANDILE And you also left me all those years.

LULAMA I left you because I had to. Do you think my husband would have accepted you? He would have killed me if I had come to his home with another man's child. My going to find work in Durban was bad enough – even though he knew I was forced to because he was not bringing us any money . . . 1958 . . . [*pause*] That was a difficult year for me. Then something happened, I bumped into an old friend that I grew up with here. Dudu looked so happy and beautiful and I could see that she had a good job.

ZANDILE She was a teacher?

LULAMA No, she was a singer with a successful group called 'Mtateni Queens', and one of their singers had just left the band, so Dudu asked me if I would like to join so I joined the group.

ZANILE [*Holding back laughter*] Haai bo wena!

LULAMA Yes, before Dudu left here we used to sing together for all the weddings, we were quite famous around here. There would never be a wedding without us singing. [*Does a bit of wedding song*]

ZANDILE I wish I could have seen that.

LULAMA I thought I could earn better money, but it was hard work.

ZANDILE Harder work than here?

LULAMA [*Laughs*] Oho! Much harder and I had to send my money back to the Transkei for the children.

ZANDILE Why did you stay then?

LULAMA I stayed, hoping for better things to come, but they didn't. That is why I have learnt not to live on hopes, that is why I am teaching you to work. The sun is going down, it's time to cook supper. Run and start the fire. I'll call you back when the bundles are ready.

As Lulama mimes gathering the bundles, she starts to sing Mgewundini, a song she used to sing when she was on the cabaret circuit. As she picks up the last bundle, she stands and arches her back, and tries to rub away the pain.

ANGELA	MAXINE
16	16
Northern	Northern

Like a Virgin
Gordon Steel

First performed by the Hull Truck Theatre Company at the Dovecote Arts Centre, Stockton-on-Tees, in 1995, at the Edinburgh Festival and then on a nationwide tour. It is set in Middlesbrough.

ANGELA and her friend MAXINE are besotted with Madonna. They play truant from school, form a band, have numerous boyfriends and dream of becoming famous very soon. Then ANGELA becomes unwell. The doctor diagnoses Myeloid Leukaemia and she is put on chemotherapy. She is warned she may lose her hair and buys herself a Madonna-style wig.

This early scene is set in the toilets of the Madison nightclub. ANGELA holds a bottle of Diamond White which she drinks though a straw, as she waits for MAXINE.

Published by Oberon Books, London

ANGELA Maxine, what are you doin'?

MAXINE I'm shakin' me lettuce.

ANGELA Aw come out Maxine, you've been in there ages.

MAXINE So.

ANGELA It bloody stinks in here. Are you havin' a shit?

MAXINE Don't be so bloody simple, you know I never have a shit when I'm out.

ANGELA What?

MAXINE You know what I mean. I can't shit anywhere unless I'm in our house.

ANGELA Well what the hell 'ave you been doing in there all this time? Making your will?

MAXINE [*Bursting into tears*] It's him. It's that bastard Jamie Power. 'E's gone off with Shirley Windows. He had three dances with me. I even bought him a drink.

ANGELA Aw come on, Maxine. Look, there's no one in here now. Oway, sort yourself out in the mirror before anybody comes in.

MAXINE Are you sure there's nobody there?

ANGELA No, hurry up.

MAXINE Right. [*She appears with face covered in tear-stained mascara*]

ANGELA Come on Maxine don't go upsetting yourself. Not over Jamie Powers.

MAXINE But I love him.

ANGELA You don't. You know you don't.

MAXINE I do. I do. I love everything about him. I love his mam. I love his Escort and the scar going down his left cheek. I just love him. What's he doin' with that little tart when he could have me? I'm gorgeous. Why did he do it to me?

ANGELA He's a twat. 'Ave nowt to do with him.

MAXINE But I love him.

ANGELA Yeah I know you do, but if you really want to get him you have to ignore him.

MAXINE But I love him.

ANGELA Treat him mean, keep him keen.

MAXINE He's sexy. Look at the state of me face.

ANGELA There's nowt I can do about that.

MAXINE Me make-up you cheeky cow. Look at it, it's exploded. Bloody hell.

ANGELA Right Maxy baby. We are gonna go out and take this place by storm.

MAXINE We are?

ANGELA We certainly are. We'll show that turd what he's missing. Who the hell is Shirley Windows? She's a right doyle.

MAXINE Yeah you're right. I'm too good for him.

ANGELA Course you are.

MAXINE I'll make him squirm.

ANGELA Course you will.

MAXINE Who does he think he is?

ANGELA He's a nobody. He's about as exciting as . . . as . . . *Going for Gold*. It's his loss.

MAXINE I'll show him exactly what he's not going to have.

ANGELA Are you ready?

MAXINE You bet your vacant personality I am.

ANGELA Well, let's go.

They perform an elaborate dance routine and then explode out of the toilet.

SALLY	HELEN
20s	16
Lancashire	Lancashire

Love on the Dole
Ronald Gow and Walter Greenwood

First performed at the Manchester Repertory Company theatre in 1934 and in London at the Garrick Theatre in 1935. It is set in Hankey Park, Salford, Lancashire.

In Hankey Park in the 1930s, unemployment is high. Mr Hardcastle is on the dole and his wife takes in washing. Their son, Harry, earns 17 shillings a week in a machine shop at the local foundry, but already many of his fellow workers have been laid off. He is courting HELEN, a local girl and they are planning to get married.

A year later, Harry has lost his job, the Public Assistance Committee have cut his dole and to make matters worse, HELEN is pregnant.

In this scene HELEN appears in the doorway of the Hardcastle's house. She is weeping. SALLY invites her inside, closing the door behind her.

Published by Samuel French, London

HELEN Can I speak to you, Sal?

SALLY Come inside, Helen.

HELEN [*Closes the door*] Are they all out?

[*Drum and singing soften. Crowd noises almost cease*]

SALLY Yes, there's only me. I'm worried about Larry. He's gone with the procession, and I'm sure the lad's ill. Well, young woman, what is it? So you're crying too, are you?

HELEN [*Sits R of the table*] I know what you're going to say. You're going to call me names and say it's my fault –

SALLY [*Comes to R of Helen*] Well, I wasn't going to congratulate you, Helen, but I'm not going to call you names.

HELEN I don't care what people say. I love Harry, and Harry loves me –

SALLY That's the spirit, lass. That's the way to talk. What are you crying for, then, if you feel that way?

HELEN They've turned me out.

SALLY Well, they've turned our Harry out, too, so there's a pair of you. [*She looks in the direction of the window*]

HELEN Harry? You mean we can't live here?

SALLY No, Dad won't have you. You see, we're so respectable in North Street, though you wouldn't think it sometimes.

HELEN But what are we going to do?

SALLY Well, now you're asking. I'm sorry, Helen. Don't cry, lass. You're not the only one as doesn't know where to turn. I'll do what I can for you.

HELEN Where's Harry?

SALLY Harry? He's carrying a banner in the demonstration. And he'll be finding a home in a prison cell if he's not careful.

HELEN If only we could find a room somewhere. I don't care where it is. You see, I've got my job at mill and we could live on that if someone'd take us in. But nobody'll take us in, nobody decent, 'cause we're not married, and we've no money for that.

SALLY I wonder how much longer us women'll take to learn that living and loving's all a damn swindle? [*She looks at the window R*] Love's all right on the pictures, but love on the dole ain't quite same thing.

HELEN I won't give up Harry.

[*Drum, singing and crowd die right out*]

SALLY [*Moves to top of the table and sits on it*] I'm not asking you to. I reckon that's all part of swindle. We *can't* give 'em up, else wouldn't we have a bit o' sense and do without love same as we do without fine clothes, and motor-cars and champagne? Would we bring children into Hanky Park if we weren't blasted lunatics?

HELEN If I'd only known this was going to happen – [*She breaks down a little*]

SALLY [*Taking both of Helen's hands*]. Aw, go on, Helen. Look at the silver lining. When you're married they'll be bound to give you money at the workhouse. And Harry'll stand a better chance of getting a job when he's wed.

HELEN Yes, but – we can't get married. We've no money for that.

SALLY [*Producing some notes from her stocking*] Let's see, is it seven and six? Or is that a dog licence? Marriage licences last for ever, though, so it's cheaper than keeping dogs. I know some marriages that wouldn't last long if you had to take out a new licence every year. [*She gives Helen a ten-shilling note*]

HELEN Oh, Sally. [*About to return the note*]

SALLY Here, take it before I change me mind.

HELEN Oh, thanks, Sally, thanks. [*She bursts into tears on Sally's knee*]

SALLY That's all right. If you feel as grateful in ten years' time, you can pay me back. You know where the Registrar's office is – in Mill Street? And don't forget to take Harry with you.

HELEN [*tearfully*] No. What shall I say?

SALLY Say you want to get married, of course. They can't eat you.

HELEN It's not what I'd planned. I always thought I'd be married in a church.

[*Crowd noises start*]

SALLY Aw. Plans are like that. If we'd any sense, we wouldn't make any.

[*She hears the crowd. She and Helen rise and go near the R door*]

HELEN Well, good-bye, Sally. And – you're awfully nice. [*She kisses Sally impulsively*]

SALLY That's all right, Helen. And don't worry yourself. Things'll be all right. [*She looks through the window*] I wish I knew what was going on down there.

HELEN I'm going to see where Harry is.

[*She opens the door and goes out*]

STEPHANIE   LOUISE
27   17

A Lovely Day Tomorrow
Ellen Dryden

First performed at the Birmingham Repertory Studio Theatre in
1983.

The action takes place in a Midlands town, where a small fringe
theatre group are performing a devised play, *Women at War*. At the
climax of their play the actors dramatise moments in recent
Midlands history – women's roles in the Second World War and most
importantly, the Coventry Blitz of 1940.

Personal responsibility is central to the play. The group consists of
Muriel, an actress recently returned to the profession after her
husband has divorced her; Annie, involved in a casual relationship
with Nick, who couldn't care less about her or anyone else; David,
ironic and somewhat detached from the rest of the cast; and
STEPHANIE, who is usually cheerful and outgoing, but bickers with
David.

At the opening of the play the cast are arriving at the Hall for
rehearsal. STEPHANIE is trying on her 1940s gear. In the middle of
the turmoil a young girl arrives: she is wearing jeans and an anorak
and stands watching the rehearsal. She goes over to speak to Nick.
At first he doesn't recognise her, then gradually he realises who she is
and introduces her to the cast as LOUISE, the daughter he hasn't seen
since she was a baby. Annie asks what he proposes to do about her.
Nick doesn't know – she's not his responsibility.

In this scene the Hall is full of props and costumes – *Women at
War* is opening that evening. STEPHANIE is sitting cleaning an old
rifle. An ATS jacket is slung over the back of her chair and there's a
large tin of Brasso and a yellow duster on the floor. After a moment
LOUISE comes in, hands deep in her anorak pockets.

Published by First Writes Books, Cambridge

STEPHANIE [*Without looking up*] Hello. You looking for Nick?

LOUISE Not specially.

Stephanie pulls back the bolt of the rifle and raises it to her shoulder.

LOUISE Is that a real gun?

STEPHANIE [*Inspecting it*] I don't honestly know. Nick does the props . . . I suppose it is. [*She looks at it dubiously*] It's bloody heavy.

LOUISE What's it for?

STEPHANIE Killing people. [*She levels the gun at Louise*] Shouldn't do that. Even in fun. Even if it's a toy gun . . . [*She lowers it. Louise is impassive. Louise picks up the ATS jacket*]

LOUISE Is this yours?

STEPHANIE Yes. That is I *wear* it . . . There's a scene on the anti-aircraft battery in the second act.

Louise puts the jacket on. It is oddly too big for her and hangs limply and awkwardly from her shoulders.

STEPHANIE [*Tartly*] You'd have been wearing that for real if you'd been born forty years sooner.

LOUISE My Gran was in the war . . . In the . . . Navy . . .

Her voice tails away as if she wonders if she has said something stupid.

STEPHANIE A Wren. Yes. Tell her to come and see the show.

LOUISE She's dead now.

Pause. Stephanie stares thoughtfully at the gun.

STEPHANIE Yes . . . the women were right in the thick of it . . . you know . . . no messing about . . . they *mattered* . . . whoever they were. The Officer in charge of the first Battery to shoot down a German plane said the women were infinitely better than the men on the instruments they were manning . . . They were on the ack ack guns too . . .

There is a kind of wistful enthusiasm for the prospect in her voice.

They were always keen to go into action . . . Even Churchill had to give way and allow them to be called 'Gunners' after he'd seen them in action. 'A fit woman can fire a rifle better than an unfit man' . . . somebody or other said . . . People don't realise what an amazing contribution –

Louise wanders aimlessly round the set looking at things with a slightly puzzled air. Stephanie watches her.

LOUISE You take all this stuff around with you?

STEPHANIE Yes. In the van.

There is a pause.

91

LOUISE Do you live anywhere?

STEPHANIE [*Amused*] Yes. I share a flat in Shepherd's Bush. My mum and dad live in Croydon. I've got a sister still at home. Why?

LOUISE Just wondered. You don't go round all the time then?

STEPHANIE No. It varies. Depends what we're doing. Do you fancy joining us?

LOUISE No. I'm no good at anything . . .

STEPHANIE Funny to think you're Nick's daughter.

LOUISE Why?

STEPHANIE Can't imagine Nick married. And he's not very fatherly.

LOUISE Well he did pack it in when I was eighteen months old. Is that blonde woman his girlfriend?

STEPHANIE Ye – es. In a way. No, not really. I don't honestly know.

LOUISE My mum can't stand him. Don't think she's seen him for fifteen years. But she still hates him.

STEPHANIE Why?

LOUISE Well, she's got nothing better to do really. Terry's dead boring.

STEPHANIE Did you go home last night?

LOUISE Yes.

STEPHANIE Shouldn't you be at work today?

LOUISE Yes. Told them I'd got 'flu.

STEPHANIE Are you going to see the show?

LOUISE I might.

STEPHANIE Why did you come back?

LOUISE I was interested.

STEPHANIE In Nick?

LOUISE Yes. And the rest of you.

STEPHANIE Well, look, you'd better keep out of everybody's way today. Especially Nick's. We all get a bit edgy when we're opening a new show and this is only the third time we've done this one. It's a funny set up here – and Nick's got a nasty temper when he likes.

LOUISE Do you like him?

STEPHANIE Yes.

LOUISE He looks a bit young.

STEPHANIE What for?

LOUISE [*With a grin*] For thirty-eight . . .

STEPHANIE We're going the day after tomorrow of course.

LOUISE Where to?

STEPHANIE Why? Do you want to follow us?

LOUISE No. I shan't bother again . . . Do many people come to this play you're doing?

STEPHANIE Varies. We'll be pretty full tonight.

LOUISE It's about the war?

STEPHANIE Yes.

LOUISE Why?

Stephanie is temporarily thrown by this.

STEPHANIE Why? Because – we think we've got something to say about the war that's – relevant to now. [*Louise is impassive*] We do a lot of – sort of political – stuff about ordinary people in crisis situations, especially women . . . And the war was something that stole six years out of everybody's lives – if they survived that is. That's something we don't have to face – not in the same way . . . We wanted to show how people faced up to that and fought back. Coped. Ordinary people. Not the Establishment . . . And it was quite a turning point for women too . . . they had to take part. Work. Run things. It was a vital stage of our liberation in many ways. Except things slipped back badly afterwards.

LOUISE But it was ages ago.

STEPHANIE Yes. But we can understand ourselves and our present struggles much better if we have an understanding of the historical processes that brought us where we are now.

Louise is unconvinced.

LOUISE They have stacks of war films on the telly.

STEPHANIE [*Drily*] That's not quite what we're aiming at.

LOUISE Are you Communists?

STEPHANIE [*Taking a deep breath. With a grin*] No.

LOUISE Mum said you probably were. Where's the loo?

STEPHANIE Down the corridor. Through the doors. On the left.

Louise goes out.

MISS MACKAY
middle-aged
Edinburgh Scots

JEAN BRODIE
early middle-age
Edinburgh Scots

The Prime of Miss Jean Brodie

Jay Presson Allen
Adapted from the novel by Muriel Spark

First presented at the Wyndham's Theatre, London in 1966 and at the Helen Hayes Theatre, New York in 1968. The action takes place in Edinburgh, Scotland from 1931 to 1938.

JEAN BRODIE, a spinster whose fiancé was killed in World War I, is an English teacher at the Marcia Blaine Academy. Many of her colleagues disapprove of her unconventional teaching methods, but she is popular among the girls, particularly her special students who become known as the 'Brodie Set'. She becomes involved with the art teacher, Teddy Lloyd and then the new music teacher, Gordon Lowther. The Headmistress, MISS MACKAY, is concerned by the increasing rumours about MISS BRODIE and the precocity of the 'Brodie Set'. She calls MISS BRODIE to her office.

At the opening of this scene MISS MACKAY is alone in her office. She is somewhat distracted and is tapping a pencil against the desktop. There is a knock at the door. MISS MACKAY straightens up and adjusts her face. MISS BRODIE enters with a poised smile.

Published by Samuel French Inc., New York

BRODIE [*Glancing at her watch*] I hope I'm not late. [*A pause*] Or early.

MACKAY No! It's 4:15 precisely. You are most punctilious. Thank you for finding the time. Please sit down. My, my! You do wear such *stimulating* colours.

BRODIE My credo is stimulate, enliven, uplift.

MACKAY No doubt. But the Marcia Blaine School is essentially conservative and any conservative school must turn out pupils who can read and write and add up. [*Smiles*] I have observed, Miss Brodie, some of your girls counting on their fingers.

BRODIE [*Also smiling*] Miss Mackay, have you summoned me to your eyrie to suggest that I am unqualified to impart the mysteries of multiplication?

MACKAY Certainly not. [*She continues to smile, refusing to seem intolerant*] I merely want to point out that we are not what, I believe, is called a progressive school. We do not encourage the – uh – progressive attitudes. Now I have noticed, Miss Brodie, a – a spirit of precocity among your girls. Your special girls.

BRODIE [*Quickly blocking Mackay's move*] Why, *thank you*. I am in my prime and my girls are benefiting from it. I am proud to think that my girls are perhaps more – aware.

MACKAY [*Pouncing*] Precisely.

BRODIE [*Before Mackay can pursue this line of thought*] To me education is a leading out. The word education comes from the root 'ex' meaning 'out' and 'duco', 'I lead'. To me, education is simply a leading out of what is already there.

MACKAY [*Dryly*] I had hoped there might also be a certain amount of putting *in*.

BRODIE [*Bravely, foolishly, plunging on*] That would not be education but intrusion. From the root prefix 'in' meaning 'in' and the stem 'trudo', 'I thrust'. Ergo to thrust a lot of information into a pupil's head.

MACKAY [*Sighs deeply*] To discuss education with such a dedicated teacher is always instructive. But it was not for that I asked you to come here. Miss Brodie. [*Directly*] I am told that you make weekly expeditions to Cramond.

BRODIE Yes. Isn't it a lovely spot?

MACKAY It is indeed. I believe Mr Lowther inherited the estate from his mother. He has lived there all his life. Overprotected, perhaps. He is not a worldly man. Not a reckless man. I doubt if he would even recognize recklessness in others. And recklessness is an indulgence which we at Marcia Blaine must eschew. Not only within our walls, but in the personal life – the conduct, as it were – of our teaching staff.

[*A moment of silence. Then gently, Brodie speaks*]

BRODIE I do not believe I have ever fully appreciated the taxing load of trivia with which a headmistress must concern herself.

MACKAY With which we must both concern ourselves. Appearances must be considered. Your – visits to Cramond Sunday after Sunday might invite ungenerous gossip in that small community.

BRODIE I must confess I am astonished, astonished that anyone,

anyone at all, might misconstrue my visits to Cramond. I am always chaperoned by my girls. Miss Mackay, I do not believe that you would ever give serious attention to the ignorant gossip of ignorant people. It is on your good judgment both as an administrator and as a *woman* that I must rely, that I *do* rely.

MACKAY [*Dryly*] I appreciate your confidence in me, Miss Brodie, but I am responsible to my school's Board of Governors.

BRODIE I flatter myself that I am not unknown to the board – having been a member of the staff of Marcia Blaine some six years prior to *your* engagement. I feel quite safe in saying that no *member of the board* has *ever* shown anything but approval and appreciation of my teaching methods. [*Laughs lightly*] Miss Mackay. I *use* Cramond. As I use anything that can possibly be of benefit to my girls. I use the woods of Cramond for lessons in botany . . . the rocks of the shore to investigate the mysteries of geology . . . It was from Cramond that Agricola's fleet set sail for the first circumnavigation of Britain. It should be patently clear to the Board of Governors that my expeditions there are expeditions for enrichment – enrichment both for my girls and for Marcia Blaine. [*Gives a brilliant smile*]

[*A long pause. Mackay sees that there is no present way around this mountain of security. She sighs.*]

MACKAY Well, thank you, Miss Brodie, I'm sure we've come to understand each other a good deal better.

BRODIE [*She stands, triumphant*] I am always at your command, Miss Mackay.

MACKAY [*Dryly*] Thank you. Good day, Miss Brodie.

BRODIE [*Stops to gaze at flowers*] Chrysanthemums. Such *service-able* flowers. [*A brilliant smile, exits*]

MACKAY [*She broods after Brodie, finally stirs to pick up one of several books on her desk. She opens the book and begins to search for some reference. She finds it, smiles grimly, reads aloud*] 'Educere, to lead. *Educari*, to feed.' *Ergo*, Miss Brodie, to educate does not mean to lead out – it means to *feed* – to feed *in*. [*Snaps book shut*] It would seem that your Latin is as 'progressive' as your mathematics. Now just what *is* your subject, Miss Brodie? [*There is a set and determined look on her face*]

ELIZA
18–20

MRS PEARCE
middle-aged

Pygmalion
George Bernard Shaw

A romantic comedy first produced in Vienna in 1913 and then in London the following year. It was the source of a successful American musical *My Fair Lady* in 1956 and was seen most recently at the Royal National Theatre in 2001.

Professor Henry Higgins, a professor of phonetics, boasts to his friend Colonel Pickering, that he could pass a cockney flower girl off as a duchess by teaching her to speak properly. The girl, ELIZA DOOLITTLE, calls at Higgins' house and asks him to give her lessons. He takes her on as his pupil and she finally emerges as a beautiful and sensitive woman.

In this scene ELIZA has only just arrived. Higgins arranges for his housekeeper, MRS PEARCE to take charge of her. She can sleep in the spare bedroom, but first of all she must have a bath.

Published by Penguin Books, London

MRS PEARCE I will have to put you here. This will be your bedroom.

LIZA O-h, I couldn't sleep here, missus. It's too good for the likes of me. I should be afraid to touch anything. I ain't a duchess yet, you know.

MRS PEARCE You have got to make yourself as clean as the room: then you won't be afraid of it. And you must call me Mrs Pearce, not missus. [*She throws open the door of the dressing-room, now modernised as a bathroom*]

LIZA Gawd! What's this? Is this where you wash clothes? Funny sort of copper I call it.

MRS PEARCE It is not a copper. This is where we wash ourselves, Eliza, and where I am going to wash you.

LIZA You expect me to get into that and wet myself all over! Not me. I should catch my death. I knew a woman did it every Saturday night; and she died of it.

MRS PEARCE Mr Higgins has the gentlemen's bathroom downstairs; and he has a bath every morning, in cold water.

LIZA Ugh! He's made of iron, that man.

MRS PEARCE If you are to sit with him and the Colonel and be taught you will have to do the same. They won't like the smell of you if you don't. But you can have the water as hot as you like. There are two taps: hot and cold.

LIZA [*weeping*] I couldn't. I dursn't. It's not natural: it would kill me. I've never had a bath in my life: not what you'd call a proper one.

MRS PEARCE Well, don't you want to be clean and sweet and decent, like a lady? You know you can't be a nice girl inside if you're a dirty slut outside.

LIZA Boohoo!!!!

MRS PEARCE Now stop crying and go back into your room and take off all your clothes. Then wrap yourself in this [*Taking down a gown from its peg and handing it to her*] and come back to me, I will get the bath ready.

LIZA [*All tears*] I can't. I won't. I'm not used to it. I've never took off all my clothes before. It's not right: it's not decent.

MRS PEARCE Nonsense, child. Don't you take off all your clothes every night when you go to bed?

LIZA [*Amazed*] No. Why should I? I should catch my death. Of course I take off my skirt.

MRS PEARCE Do you mean that you sleep in the underclothes you wear in the daytime?

LIZA What else have I to sleep in?

MRS PEARCE You will never do that again as long as you live here. I will get you a proper nightdress.

LIZA Do you mean change into cold things and lie awake shivering half the night? You want to kill me, you do.

MRS PEARCE I want to change you from a frowzy slut to a clean respectable girl fit to sit with the gentlemen in the study. Are you going to trust me and do what I tell you or be thrown out and sent back to your flower basket?

LIZA But you don't know what the cold is to me. You don't know how I dread it.

MRS PEARCE Your bed won't be cold here: I will put a hot water bottle in it. [*Pushing her into the bedroom*] Off with you and undress.

LIZA Oh, if only I'd a known what a dreadful thing it is to be clean I'd never have come. I didn't know when I was well off. I –

[*Mrs Pearce pushes her through the door, but leaves it partly open lest her prisoner should take to flight*]

Mrs Pearce puts on a pair of white rubber sleeves, and fills the bath, mixing hot and cold, and testing the result with the bath thermometer. She perfumes it with a handful of bath salts and adds a palmful of mustard. She then takes a formidable-looking, long-handled scrubbing brush and soaps it profusely with a ball of scented soap.

Eliza comes back with nothing on but the bath gown huddled tightly round her, a piteous spectacle of abject terror.

MRS PEARCE Now come along. Take that thing off.

LIZA Oh I couldn't, Mrs Pearce: I reely couldn't. I never done such a thing.

MRS PEARCE Nonsense. Here: step in and tell me whether it's hot enough for you.

LIZA Ah-oo! Ah-oo! It's too hot.

MRS PEARCE [*Deftly snatching the gown away and throwing Eliza down on her back*] It won't hurt you. [*She sets to work with the scrubbing brush*]

Eliza's screams are heartrending.

LUCY   MELINDA
young   young

The Recruiting Officer
George Farquhar

This Restoration comedy was first performed at the Theatre Royal, Drury Lane in 1706 and is based on Farquhar's own experience as a recruiting officer in Shrewsbury.

Captain Plume recruits his grenadiers by courting their sweethearts and wives. His sergeant, Kite, even poses as an astrologer to persuade the gullible to serve Her Majesty.

Early in the play, Captain Plume and his friend Worthy, a gentleman of Shropshire meet to discuss what can be done about their respective lovers. Silvia, who was about to fall into Plume's embraces, has become heiress to her father's estate and MELINDA, the love of Worthy's life, has inherited a large fortune. Both girls are determined not to be undervalued and are now treating their lovers with marked disdain.

Plume decides to take a market woman, Rose, as his mistress to teach Silvia a lesson. Worthy arranges for MELINDA to meet a fortune-teller – in the person of the disguised Sergeant Kite – who describes Worthy in detail and warns her she will die a maid.

In this scene MELINDA is pouring out her heart to her maid, LUCY.

Published by *New Mermaids*, A & C Black, London

MELINDA 'Tis the greatest misfortune in nature for a woman to want a confidante: we are so weak that we can do nothing without assistance, and then a secret racks us worse than the colic; I'm at this minute so sick of a secret that I'm ready to faint away – help me, Lucy.

LUCY Bless me, madam, what's the matter?

MELINDA Vapours only – I begin to recover – if Silvia were in town, I could heartily forgive her faults for the ease of discovering my own.

LUCY You're thoughtful, madam; am not I worthy to know the cause?

MELINDA You're a servant, and a secret would make you saucy.

LUCY Not unless you should find fault without a cause, madam.

MELINDA Cause or not cause, I must not lose the pleasure of chiding when I please; women must discharge their vapours somewhere, and before we get husbands, our servants must expect to bear with 'em.

LUCY Then, madam, you had better raise me to a degree above a servant: you know my family, and that five hundred pound would set me upon the foot of a gentlewoman, and make me worthy the confidence of any lady in the land. Besides, madam, 'twill extremely encourage me in the great design I now have in hand.

MELINDA I don't find that your design can be of any great advantage to you; 'twill please me indeed, in the humour I have of being revenged on the fool for his vanity of making love to me, so I don't much care if I do promise you five hundred pound upon my day of marriage.

LUCY That is the way, madam, to make me diligent in the vocation of a confidante, which I think is generally to bring people together.

MELINDA Oh, Lucy, I can hold my secret no longer – you must know that hearing of the famous fortune-teller in town, I went disguised to satisfy a curiosity which has cost me dear; that fellow is certainly the devil, or one of his bosom favourites, he has told me the most surprising things of my past life –

LUCY Things past, madam, can hardly be reckoned surprising, because we know them already; did he tell you anything surprising that was to come?

MELINDA One thing very surprising, he said I should die a maid.

LUCY Die a maid! Come into the world for nothing! – Dear madam, if you should believe him, it might come to pass; for the bare thought on't might kill one in four and twenty hours. – And did you ask him any questions about me?

MELINDA You! Why, I passed for you.

LUCY So 'tis I that am to die a maid – but the devil was a liar from the beginning, he can't make me die a maid – I have put it out of his power already.

MELINDA I do but jest, I would have passed for you, and called myself Lucy, but he presently told me my name, my quality, my fortune, and gave me the whole history of my life; he told me of a lover I had in this country, and described Worthy exactly, but in nothing so well as in his present indifference – I fled to him for refuge here today – he never so much as encouraged me in my fright, but coldly told me that he was sorry for the accident, because it might give the town cause to censure my conduct; excused his not waiting on me home, made me a careless bow, and walked off. 'Sdeath, I could have stabbed him, or myself, 'twas the same thing. – Yonder he comes – I will so slave him.

LUCY Don't exasperate him, consider what the fortune-teller told you; men are scarce, and as times go, it is not impossible for a woman to die a maid.

BLANCHE	STELLA
30	25
American/Mississippi	American/Mississippi

A Streetcar Named Desire
Tennessee Williams

First produced in London at the Aldwych Theatre in 1949 and directed by Laurence Olivier. The action takes place in a two-storey corner building in New Orleans.

School teacher BLANCHE DUBOIS comes to stay with her sister, STELLA and her husband, Stanley Kowalski in the slums of Elysian Fields, New Orleans.

In this opening scene BLANCHE is alone in the flat waiting for STELLA to return from the local bowling alley. She sits in a chair very stiffly with her shoulders slightly hunched. She notices something in a half-opened closet, springs up, crosses to it and removes a whisky bottle. She pours a half tumbler of whisky and tosses it down, carefully replacing the bottle and washing out the tumbler in the sink. Then she resumes her seat in front of the table.

Published by Penguin Books, London

BLANCHE Stella! What have you heard about me?
STELLA Huh?
BLANCHE What have people been telling you about me?
STELLA Telling?
BLANCHE You haven't heard any – unkind – gossip about me?
STELLA Why, no, Blanche, of course not!
BLANCHE Honey, there was – a good deal of talk in Laurel.
STELLA About *you*, Blanche?
BLANCHE I wasn't so good the last two years or so, after Belle Reve had started to slip through my fingers.
STELLA All of us do things we –
BLANCHE I never was hard or self-sufficient enough. When people are soft – soft people have got to court the favour of hard ones,

Stella. Have got to be seductive – put on soft colours, the colours of butterfly wings, and glow – make a little – temporary magic just in order to pay for – one night's shelter! That's why I've been – not so awf'ly good lately. I've run for protection, Stella, from under one leaky roof to another leaky roof – because it was storm – all storm, and I was – caught in the centre . . . People don't see you – *men* don't – don't even admit your existence unless they are making love to you. And you've got to have your existence admitted by someone, if you're going to have someone's protection. And so the soft people have got to – shimmer and glow – put a – paper lantern over the light . . . But I'm scared now – awf'ly scared. I don't know how much longer I can turn the trick. It isn't enough to be soft. You've got to be soft *and attractive.* And I – I'm fading now!

[*The afternoon has faded to dusk. Stella holds a bottled soft drink in her hand.*]

Have you been listening to me?

STELLA I don't listen to you when you are being morbid! [*She advances with the bottled coke*]

BLANCHE [*With abrupt change to gaiety*]: Is that coke for me?

STELLA Not for anyone else!

BLANCHE Why, you precious thing, you! Is it just coke?

STELLA [*Turning*] You mean you want a shot in it!

BLANCHE Well, honey, a shot never does a coke any harm! Let me? You mustn't wait on me!

STELLA I like to wait on you, Blanche. It makes it seem more like home. [*She finds a glass, and pours a shot of whisky into it*]

BLANCHE I have to admit I love to be waited on . . .

[*Stella goes to her with the glass. Blanche suddenly clutches Stella's free hand with a moaning sound and presses the hand to her lips. Stella is embarrassed by her show of emotion. Blanche speaks in a choked voice*]

You're – you're – so *good* to me! And I –

STELLA Blanche.

BLANCHE I know, I won't! You hate me to talk sentimental. But honey, *believe* I feel things more than I *tell* you! I *won't* stay long! I won't, I *promise* I –

STELLA Blanche!

BLANCHE [*Hysterically*] I won't, I promise, *I'll* go! Go *soon*! I will *really*! I *won't* hang around until he – throws me out . . .

STELLA Now will you stop talking foolish?

BLANCHE Yes, honey. Watch how you pour – that fizzy stuff foams over!

[*Blanche laughs shrilly and grabs the glass, but her hand shakes so it almost slips from her grasp. Stella pours the coke into the glass. It foams over and spills. Blanch gives a piercing cry*]

STELLA [*Shocked by the cry*] Heavens!

BLANCHE Right on my pretty white skirt!

STELLA Oh . . . Use my hanky. Blot gently.

BLANCHE [*Slowly recovering*] I know – gently – gently . . .

STELLA Did it stain?

BLANCHE Not a bit. Ha-ha! Isn't that lucky? [*She sits down shakily, taking a grateful drink. She holds the glass in both hands and continues to laugh a little*]

STELLA Why did you scream like that?

BLANCHE I don't know why I screamed! [*Continuing nervously*] Mitch – Mitch is coming at seven. I guess I am just feeling nervous about our relations. [*She begins to talk rapidly and breathlessly*] He hasn't gotten a thing but a good-night kiss, that's all I have given him, Stella. I want his respect. And men don't want anything they get too easy. But on the other hand men lose interest quickly. Especially when the girl is over – thirty. They think a girl over thirty ought to – the vulgar term is – 'put out' . . . And I – I'm not 'putting out'. Of course he – he doesn't know – I mean I haven't informed him – of my real age!

STELLA Why are you sensitive about your age?

BLANCHE Because of hard knocks my vanity's been given. What I mean is – he thinks I'm sort of – prim and proper, you know! [*She laughs out sharply*] I want to *deceive* him enough to make him – want me . . .

STELLA Blanche, do you want *him*?

BLANCHE I want to *rest*! I want to breathe quietly again! Yes – I *want* Mitch . . . *very badly*! Just think! If it happens! I can leave here and not be anyone's problem . . .

STELLA [*Kissing Blanche impulsively*] It *will* happen!

BLANCHE [*Doubtfully*] It will?

STELLA It *will*! [*She goes across into the kitchen, looking back at Blanche*] It will, honey, *it will* . . . but don't take another drink!

[*Her voice catches as she goes out of the door to meet her husband*]

VARVARA   OLGA
27   35

Summerfolk

Maxim Gorky
A new version by Nick Dear

This version was first performed in the Olivier auditorium of the National Theatre in 1999.

In the early 20th century, Russians of every social class were beginning to sense the onset of a great upheaval. A diverse group of Russians meet, as they do every year, at their Summer holiday retreat. Some are frightened at the prospect of change, some are angry and some yearn for a new life. As they question the value of their work, their art and their leisure, relationships break under the strain and scandals of business and infidelity are laid bare.

This scene takes place in the early evening, as OLGA strolls along the path towards her friend VARVARA's dacha and meets her coming out onto the terrace. VARVARA invites her in, but OLGA prefers to stay outside. Almost immediately she starts complaining about her husband, the overworked doctor Dudakov, 'running away from family life'. Prone to exaggeration she works herself up into a frenzy, finally insulting VARVARA.

Note: 'dacha' – Russian country cottage used especially in summer

Published by Faber & Faber, London

OLGA [*quietly*] Well. Have you any idea why he's like that?
VARVARA No. Nor do I wish to. Coming in?
OLGA Stay outside with me. They'll manage without you.
VARVARA I'm sure. – You seem flustered again.
OLGA How could I not be? He dashes back from town, spends two minutes with the children, then dashes out again! Hardly guaranteed to make me leap for joy, is it?

They wander towards the trees.

VARVARA He's at our house.

OLGA He's running away from family life, that's what he's doing. I know, I know, he's overworked, he needs a break, but what about me? Don't I get a break? I work myself into the ground! And nothing I can do or say is right. Lord! It makes me livid! He needs reminding that I've sacrificed my youth, my looks, everything – all for him!

VARVARA [*Gently*] Dear Olga . . . you do like a moan, don't you?

From indoors comes the sound of an argument, increasing in volume.

OLGA Well, what if I do? I feel I should say to him: I'm going away! Taking the children and going away!

VARVARA That's a splendid idea. Give yourselves a rest from each other. Make the arrangements, I'll lend you the money.

OLGA I owe you too much already!

VARVARA It's nothing. Let's try and calm down a little. Come, sit.

OLGA I hate myself for not being able to manage without your help. Do you think I like taking your husband's money? How can one have any self-respect, if one can't manage the household finances . . . can't get by without hand-outs? Well? Well? Do you know there are times when I don't like you? Loathe you in fact. Can't bear you. Always so calm and rational. Never showing any real *passion*!

VARVARA But my dear, it's my way of coping. I simply don't allow myself to complain. It doesn't mean I don't feel like it!

OLGA I believe that those who are always helping others must, at the bottom of their hearts, despise the ones they're helping. Yes. And I'd like to be one of the helpers.

VARVARA So you can despise the needy?

OLGA Yes! Yes! I don't like people! Why should I like people? I don't like Maria Lvovna – who does she think she is, to judge us from on high? I don't like Ryumin. Spouts his philosophy, hasn't the guts to lift a finger. Do you think I like your husband? He's as soft as bread before you put it in the oven. And he's petrified of you. That's a great example, that is! And as for your brother, who's in love with the shrew Lvovna –

VARVARA [*Surprised*] Olga! What has come over you? That's not nice at all!

OLGA So? And Kaleria – arrogant hussy. Claims to be searching for truth and beauty – really looking for a man to take her to bed!

VARVARA Olga! Stop this! You shouldn't allow yourself to . . . These are dark places, Olga, dark!

OLGA [*Softly, but maliciously*] I do not care. I do not care where we go, as long as it's away from here, this unendurable drudgery! I want to live! I'm no worse than anyone else! I've got eyes in my head, I'm not thick! I can see that even you – oh, you live very nicely thank you, your husband's made some money – not a hundred per cent honestly, either, according to what people say – you've contrived – somehow – not to tie yourself down with screaming children!

Varvara stands and stares at Olga, completely amazed.

VARVARA Contrived . . . ? What are you implying?

OLGA I don't know how you did it!

VARVARA [*Very coldly*] Did what? What do you mean?

Pause. Olga begins to squirm with embarrassment.

OLGA Not anything in particular . . . but my husband says . . . some women don't want children.

VARVARA I have no idea what you actually think. But you clearly suspect me of something base. Don't say any more.

OLGA Varya, I didn't mean it . . . Don't look at me like that . . . I'm only repeating what everyone knows about your husband . . .

VARVARA I have treated you as my sister. If I didn't know how difficult things are for you . . . If I didn't know how we used to dream, to share our dreams of another way of life . . . Oh, God!

OLGA I've said something awful, haven't I? Please, please forgive me. I'm so nasty!

VARVARA We've watched our dreams disintegrate, wept for them together. I'm very hurt, Olga. Have you got what you wanted? [*Yells*] You hurt me!

OLGA Don't be like that, Varya!

VARVARA I'm going.

Varvara moves away. Olga gets up too.

Don't follow me. Don't you dare follow me!

OLGA What, never? Can't I be with you, ever? Varya?

VARVARA I don't understand! Why have you done this to me?

SONYA
40s

ANDREY
late 40s

Afterplay
Brian Friel

First produced with *The Bear* at the Gate Theatre, Dublin in 2002, *Afterplay* revisits the lives of Andrey Prozorov and Sonya Serebriakova, who had a previous existence in two separate plays written by Anton Chekhov a hundred years ago,

These two characters came from very different backgrounds and now we meet them again, 20 years after their previous fictional lives have ended. In part ANDREY is still an only boy, confused, motherless, reared in a remote provincial town by a domineering father and three restless sisters. SONYA is still struggling to manage the family estate and is as hopelessly in love with Astrov, the local doctor, as she was all those years ago.

The action takes place in a small run-down café in Moscow in the early 1920s. It is evening and SONYA is the only customer. Then ANDREY arrives – shabbily dressed and carrying a violin case under his arm. At first she doesn't recognise him until he reminds her that they had shared a table there the evening before. He had told her then that his wife, Natasha was dead and that he was a violinist rehearsing with a big orchestra opening in La Bohème at the Opera House the following night. She had been suitably impressed and in turn told him how well she was managing her large estate. He sits down at her table and they resume their conversation of the previous evening. As he gets up to order some more tea she takes a bottle of vodka from her handbag and pours a quick drink, then pours another and puts the bottle back into her bag. When he returns with the tea he tells her he has a confession to make: his wife is still alive, but she has left him.

SONYA persuades him to take a little vodka and gradually, as they drink, their stories begin to unravel. She raises her glass to wish him success for his opening night at the Opera House.

Published by Faber & Faber, London

SONYA Anyhow – [*Toasts*] To tomorrow night and to a great, great success.

ANDREY Another little fable.

SONYA Sorry?

ANDREY No, not a fable at all. A tiny fiction. A small untruth. Of course I'm ashamed of all the untruths I've told you last night and tonight; but you'll agree most of them were trivial. But this little fiction about *La Bohème* is just that bit larger and probably unpardonable and you may feel that I have misled you shamelessly and you may decide that you cannot forgive me; and if you do I will fully understand that –

SONYA Andrey, what are you –?

ANDREY – although in self-defence I must say that the *La Bohème* fiction was not premeditated but came to me on the spur of the moment shortly after we began talking last night at that table over there; and when you told me that the yolk of a lightly boiled pheasant's egg was good for chilblains, for some bizarre reason it occurred to me at that very moment – absurd, I know, absurd, absurd – but I suddenly thought that if I said I was a violinist in an orchestra, that would sound very grand and I might impress you.

SONYA Andrey, are you telling me –?

ANDREY I'm not in any orchestra.

SONYA Not in –?

ANDREY We're on the street.

SONYA What does that mean?

ANDREY That's where we play. Outdoors.

SONYA Not in the Opera House?

ANDREY On the street.

SONYA Not in the Puccini?

ANDREY On the street.

SONYA You busk.

ANDREY You're right.

SONYA Oh my God. You were never in Puccini?

ANDREY Never.

SONYA Never in the Opera House?

ANDREY Buskers.

SONYA Where were you tonight?

ANDREY At Central Station.

SONYA And last night?

ANDREY The National Gallery – outside.

SONYA On the pavement?

ANDREY Yes.

SONYA Who is we?

ANDREY Ivan and myself.

SONYA He's a fiddler, too?

ANDREY Ivan plays the balalaika. Badly. Would it be a bit cheeky of us to play outside the Opera House tomorrow night?

SONYA Andrey –!

ANDREY Why not? Nobody knows of my association with *La Bohème* except you.

SONYA What association, in the name of God?

ANDREY None. You're right.

SONYA So that every detail you told me about the opera – one lie after another?

ANDREY Sorry. Began so innocently, too.

SONYA And the radiant Mimi and the bullying conductor and the efficient orchestra –?

ANDREY Little fictions.

SONYA Little –? Bloody lies! And the flow of blood to your precious bottom and feet – that was really touching, wasn't it?

ANDREY That's no fiction. That's true.

SONYA Why am I asking? What do I care? Lie away, for God's sake!

ANDREY You're right to be angry.

SONYA Angry? Why should I be angry? And that – that – that –?

ANDREY The suit?

SONYA That's what buskers wear, is it?

ANDREY I tell myself privately that it is a classical touch. Well, down-at-heel classical. You think it's not appropriate?

SONYA Yes! – no! maybe! – what do I know what you should wear! There isn't a busker's uniform, is there?

ANDREY You think it's inappropriate?

SONYA Andrey, honest to God I don't think I know anything any more.

ANDREY Ivan wears one, too. With a purple silk cummerbund.

SONYA The bad balalaika player?

ANDREY That was hasty. Indifferent but keen. His is slightly shabbier than mine. But then he has that splendid Uzbekistan physique, you know.

SONYA No, I don't know.

ANDREY Oh, yes. Good height, broad shoulders, straight back. He carries it magnificently, Ivan.

SONYA That makes me very happy.
ANDREY Yes, he looks just splendid.
SONYA How long will you stay here?
ANDREY Another week, maybe. Then home.
SONYA But you'll be back?
ANDREY We come here every month.
SONYA In all your classical grandeur?
ANDREY You're mocking me.
SONYA Or is this monthly visit another little fiction? I don't know what to believe any more. And I really don't care.

ELVIRA   CHARLES
20s   30s–40s

Blithe Spirit
Noel Coward

Produced at the Opera House, Manchester in 1941 and transferred to the Piccadilly Theatre, London later that year. It is set in the living room of Charles Condomine's house in Kent.

CHARLES, an author whose first wife, ELVIRA, has been dead for seven years, is now happily married to his second wife, Ruth. He is collecting material for his latest book and invites Madame Arcati, a local medium, to conduct a séance at their home. After Madame Arcati has left ELVIRA returns from 'The Other Side' and proceeds to make life extremely difficult.

In this scene she has just materialised. She is visible and audible only to CHARLES, and Ruth, who can hear only CHARLES's half of the conversation, is convinced that her husband is either mad or drunk. She refuses to listen to any more of his 'nonsense' and walks out of the room, leaving him alone with ELVIRA, who has been thoroughly enjoying Ruth's discomfort.

Published by Samuel French, London

ELVIRA That was one of the most enjoyable half-hours I have ever spent.
CHARLES [*putting down his glass on the drinks table*] Oh, Elvira – how could you!
ELVIRA Poor Ruth!
CHARLES [*staring at her*] This is obviously an hallucination, isn't it?
ELVIRA I'm afraid I don't know the technical term for it.
CHARLES [*coming down* C] What am I to do?
ELVIRA What Ruth suggested – relax.
CHARLES [*moving below the chair to the sofa*] Where have you come from?

ELVIRA Do you know, it's very peculiar, but I've sort of forgotten.

CHARLES Are you to be here indefinitely?

ELVIRA I don't know that either.

CHARLES Oh, my God!

ELVIRA Why? Would you hate it so much if I was?

CHARLES Well, you must admit it would be embarrassing?

ELVIRA I don't see why, really. It's all a question of adjusting yourself. Anyhow, I think it's horrid of you to be so unwelcoming and disagreeable.

CHARLES Now look here, Elvira –

ELVIRA [*near tears*] I do. I think you're mean.

CHARLES Try to see my point, dear. I've been married to Ruth for five years, and you've been dead for seven . . .

ELVIRA Not dead, Charles. 'Passed over.' It's considered vulgar to say 'dead' where I come from.

CHARLES Passed over, then.

ELVIRA At any rate, now that I'm here, the least you can do is to make a pretence of being amiable about it.

CHARLES Of course, my dear, I'm delighted in one way.

ELVIRA I don't believe you love me any more.

CHARLES I shall always love the memory of you.

ELVIRA [*crossing slowly above the sofa by the armchair to downstage L*] You mustn't think me unreasonable, but I really am a little hurt. You called me back; and at great inconvenience I came – and you've been thoroughly churlish ever since I arrived.

CHARLES [*gently*] Believe me, Elvira, I most emphatically did not send for you. There's been some mistake.

ELVIRA [*irritably*] Well, somebody did – and that child said it was you. I remember I was playing backgammon with a very sweet old Oriental gentleman, I think his name was Genghiz Khan, and I'd just thrown double sixes, and then the child paged me and the next thing I knew I was in this room. Perhaps it was your subconscious . . .

CHARLES You must find out whether you are going to stay or not, and we can make arrangements accordingly.

ELVIRA I don't see how I can.

CHARLES Well, try to think. Isn't there anyone that you know, that you can get in touch with over there – on the other side, or whatever it's called – who could advise you?

ELVIRA I can't think – it seems so far away – as though I'd dreamed it . . .

CHARLES You must know somebody else besides Genghiz Khan.

ELVIRA [*moving to the armchair*] Oh, Charles . . .

CHARLES What is it?

ELVIRA I want to cry, but I don't think I'm able to.

CHARLES What do you want to cry for?

ELVIRA It's seeing you again – and you being so irascible, like you always used to be.

CHARLES I don't mean to be irascible, Elvira.

ELVIRA Darling – I don't mind really – I never did.

CHARLES Is it cold – being a ghost?

ELVIRA No – I don't think so.

CHARLES What happens if I touch you?

ELVIRA I doubt if you can. Do you want to?

CHARLES [*sitting at the L end of the sofa*] Oh, Elvira . . . [*He buries his face in his hands*]

ELVIRA [*moving to the L arm of the sofa*] What is it, darling?

CHARLES I really do feel strange, seeing you again.

ELVIRA [*moving to R below the sofa and round above it again to the L arm*] That's better.

CHARLES [*looking up*] What's better?

ELVIRA Your voice was kinder.

CHARLES Was I ever unkind to you when you were alive?

ELVIRA Often.

CHARLES Oh, how can you! I'm sure that's an exaggeration.

ELVIRA Not at all. You were an absolute pig that time we went to Cornwall and stayed in that awful hotel. You hit me with a billiard cue.

CHARLES Only very, very gently.

ELVIRA I loved you very much.

CHARLES I loved you too . . . [*He puts out his hand to her and then draws it away*] No, I can't touch you. Isn't that horrible?

ELVIRA Perhaps it's as well if I'm going to stay for any length of time. [*She sits on the L arm of the sofa*]

CHARLES I suppose I shall wake up eventually . . . but I feel strangely peaceful now.

ELVIRA That's right. Put your head back.

CHARLES [*doing so*] Like that?

ELVIRA [*stroking his hair*] Can you feel anything?

CHARLES Only a very little breeze through my hair . . .

ELVIRA Well, that's better than nothing.

CHARLES [*drowsily*] I suppose if I'm really out of my mind they'll put me in an asylum.

ELVIRA Don't worry about that – just relax.

CHARLES [*very drowsily indeed*] Poor Ruth.

ELVIRA [*gently and sweetly*] To hell with Ruth.

MARGERY
young

PINCHWIFE
middle-aged

The Country Wife
William Wycherley

This Restoration Comedy was first performed in 1675, probably by
the King's Company at the Theatre Royal, Drury Lane. It is set in
London.

JACK PINCHWIFE, a middle-aged rake, has married MARGERY, a
pretty young country girl, and is determined to keep her away from
the young 'gallants' about town. He even goes as far as making her
wear her younger brother's clothes when they venture into the town.
However, at the Exchange they meet the notorious Mr Horner who
insists on kissing 'the young gentleman' and while PINCHWIFE goes
to look for the coach, lures MARGERY into one of the sidewalks.

In this scene, set in a bedchamber, PINCHWIFE questions his wife
closely about her meeting with Horner. He insists that she sits down
and writes to Horner telling him he must cease to pursue her and that
she loathes and detests him.

Published by *New Mermaids*, A & C Black, London

Note: There is not room in this book to print all scenes in their entirety, but it is well
worthwhile looking at *The Country Wife* – as you should do anyway – and perhaps
extending this duologue.

Act Four, Scene One
*The scene changes to a bedchamber, where appear Pinchwife, Mrs
Pinchwife*
PINCHWIFE Come, tell me, I say.
MRS PINCHWIFE Lord! ha'n't I told it an hundred times over?
PINCHWIFE [*Aside*] I would try if, in the repetition of the ungrateful
    tale, I could find her altering it in the least circumstance; for if her

ungrateful disagreeable

117

story be false, she is so too. – Come, how was't, baggage?

MRS PINCHWIFE Lord, what pleasure you take to hear it, sure!

PINCHWIFE No, you take more in telling it, I find. But speak – how was't?

MRS PINCHWIFE He carried me up into the house next to the Exchange.

PINCHWIFE So, and you two were only in the room.

MRS PINCHWIFE Yes, for he sent away a youth, that was there, for some dried fruit and China oranges.

PINCHWIFE Did he so? Damn him for it – and for –

MRS PINCHWIFE But presently came up the gentlewoman of the house.

PINCHWIFE Oh, 'twas well she did! But what did he do whilst the fruit came?

MRS PINCHWIFE He kissed me an hundred times, and told me he fancied he kissed my fine sister, meaning me, you know, whom he said he loved with all his soul, and bid me be sure to tell her so, and to desire her to be at her window by eleven of the clock this morning, and he would walk under it at that time.

PINCHWIFE [*Aside*] And he was as good as his word, very punctual, a pox reward him for't.

MRS PINCHWIFE Well, and he said if you were not within, he would come up to her, meaning me, you know bud, still.

PINCHWIFE [*Aside*] So – he knew her certainly. But for this confession I am obliged to her simplicity. – But what, you stood very still when he kissed you?

MRS PINCHWIFE Yes, I warrant you; would you have had me discovered myself?

PINCHWIFE But you told me he did some beastliness to you, as you called it. What was't?

MRS PINCHWIFE Why, he put –

PINCHWIFE What?

MRS PINCHWIFE Why, he put the tip of his tongue between my lips, and so muzzled me – and I said, I'd bite it.

PINCHWIFE An eternal canker seize it, for a dog!

you two were only only you two were
China oranges sweet oranges; a delicacy
whilst until
muzzled kissed closely
for a dog for behaving like a dog

MRS PINCHWIFE Nay, you need not be so angry with him neither, for to say truth he has the sweetest breath I ever knew.

PINCHWIFE The devil! You were satisfied with it then, and would do it again?

MRS PINCHWIFE Not unless he should force me.

PINCHWIFE Force you, changeling! I tell you no woman can be forced.

MRS PINCHWIFE Yes, but she may sure by such a one as he, for he's a proper, goodly strong man; 'tis hard, let me tell you, to resist him.

PINCHWIFE [*Aside*] So, 'tis plain she loves him, yet she has not love enough to make her conceal it from me. But the sight of him will increase her aversion for me, and love for him; and that love instruct her how to deceive me and satisfy him, all idiot as she is. Love! 'Twas he gave women first their craft, their art of deluding. Out of nature's hands they came plain, open, silly, and fit for slaves, as she and heaven intended 'em, but damned Love – well – I must strangle that little monster whilst I can deal with him. – Go fetch pen, ink, and paper out of the next room.

MRS PINCHWIFE Yes, bud. *Exit Mrs Pinchwife*

PINCHWIFE [*Aside*] Why should women have more invention in love than men? It can only be because they have more desires, more soliciting passions, more lust, and more of the devil.

Mrs Pinchwife returns

Come, minx, sit down and write.

MRS PINCHWIFE Ay, dear bud, but I can't do't very well.

PINCHWIFE I wish you could not at all.

MRS PINCHWIFE But what should I write for?

PINCHWIFE I'll have you write a letter to your lover.

MRS PINCHWIFE O Lord, to the fine gentleman a letter!

PINCHWIFE Yes, to the fine gentleman . . . Come, begin. [*Dictates*] 'Sir' –

MRS PINCHWIFE Shan't I say 'Dear Sir'? You know one says always something more than bare 'Sir'.

PINCHWIFE Write as I bid you, or I will write 'whore' with this penknife in your face.

changeling simpleton
plain, open straightforward, without guile
little monster Cupid
invention inventiveness
soliciting urgent

MRS PINCHWIFE Nay, good bud. [*She writes*] 'Sir'.

PINCHWIFE 'Though I suffered last night your nauseous, loathed kisses and embraces' – Write.

MRS PINCHWIFE Nay, why should I say so? You know I told you he had a sweet breath.

PINCHWIFE Write!

MRS PINCHWIFE Let me but put out 'loathed'.

PINCHWIFE Write, I say.

MRS PINCHWIFE Well, then. [*Writes*]

PINCHWIFE Let's see what you have writ. [Takes the paper and reads] 'Though I suffered last night your kisses and embraces'. – Thou impudent creature! Where is 'nauseous' and 'loathed'?

MRS PINCHWIFE I can't abide to write such filthy words.

PINCHWIFE Once more write as I'd have you, and question it not, or I will spoil thy writing with this. [*Holds up the penknife*] I will stab out those eyes that cause my mischief.

MRS PINCHWIFE O Lord, I will!

PINCHWIFE So – so – Let's see now! [*Reads*] 'Though I suffered last night your nauseous, loathed kisses and embraces'. – Go on – 'Yet I would not have you presume that you shall ever repeat them'. – So –

MRS PINCHWIFE [*She writes*] I have writ it . . .

PINCHWIFE . . . for ever more cease to pursue her, who hates and detests you' –

MRS PINCHWIFE [*She writes on. Sighs*] Soh –

PINCHWIFE What, do you sigh? – 'detests you – as much as she loves her husband and her honour'.

MRS PINCHWIFE I vow, husband, he'll ne'er believe I should write such a letter.

PINCHWIFE What, he'd expect a kinder from you? Come now, your name only.

MRS PINCHWIFE What, shan't I say 'Your most faithful, humble servant till death'?

PINCHWIFE No, tormenting fiend! [*Aside*] Her style, I find, would be very soft. – Come, wrap it up now, whilst I go fetch wax and a candle, and write on the back side 'For Master Horner'.

put out cross out
kinder more loving
style formal conclusion
soft mollifying

Exit Pinchwife

MRS PINCHWIFE 'For Master Horner' – So, I am glad he has told me his name. Dear Master Horner! But why should I send thee such a letter that will vex thee and make thee angry with me? – Well, I will not send it. – Ay, but then my husband will kill me – for I see plainly, he won't let me love Master Horner – but what care I for my husband? – I won't, so I won't send poor Master Horner such a letter – but then my husband – But oh, what if I writ at bottom, my husband made me write it? – Ay, but then my husband would see't – Can one have no shift? Ah, a London woman would have had a hundred presently. Stay – what if I should write a letter, and wrap it up like this, and write upon't too? Ay, but then my husband would see't – I don't know what to do – But yet i'vads I'll try, so I will – for I will not send this letter to poor Master Horner, come what will on't.

shift expedient

TOMMY   ROSIE
30s   mid-20s

Damsels in Distress: FlatSpin

Alan Ayckbourn

First performed at the Stephen Joseph Theatre, Scarborough in July 2001 and at the Duchess Theatre, London in September 2002. It is part of a trilogy under the heading *Damsels in Distress.*

ROSIE, a struggling young actor, is minding a luxurious riverside apartment while her uncle, the janitor, is away. When a good-looking stranger calls in from next door, she pretends to be the owner, Joanna Rupelford, and invites him in. However, what promises to be a romantic interlude turns into a nightmare. A man and woman arrive, supposedly from the Drug Squad, and coerce her into continuing to play the part of 'Joanna' in order to trap a courier bringing in the latest consignment of drugs.

In this scene ROSIE/'Joanna' is waiting for the courier to arrive. She is 'looked after' by TOMMY ANGEL, a professional bodyguard who boasts that he worked with the SAS for seven years.

Published by Faber & Faber, London

TOMMY Just you and me then, eh?
ROSIE [*A little warily*] Yes.
Tommy does a few limbering up movements.
TOMMY [*Indicating his stomach*] You want to get a feel of that?
ROSIE What?
TOMMY [*Patting his stomach again*] This. Like a fucking iron bedstead, this is.
ROSIE Great.
TOMMY Want to feel?
ROSIE No, thank you.

TOMMY [*Punching himself hard*] Iron. [*Punching himself again*] Like steel. That's all exercise, that is . . .

ROSIE What are you in now, MI5?

TOMMY MI5. You must be joking. Never in a month of Sundays.

ROSIE No?

TOMMY Wouldn't catch me there. More sense than that.

ROSIE Dangerous, is it?

TOMMY Dangerous? No, it's not dangerous. It's the pay. It's terrible. They're as mean as buggery. I tell you, I used to have a brother-in-law that was in '5. They flew him out over Easter – he missed the whole of Easter for covert operations – know what I'm saying? – they flew him out to the Middle bloody East, Operation Desert Storm going on all around him, Arabs taking shots at him, all of that – he gets back by the skin of his teeth – and he puts in, you know, naturally, for his Bank Holiday overtime – Good Friday, Easter Monday. Do you know what they told him? You are seriously not going to believe this. They told him he couldn't claim because he wasn't technically speaking in a Christian country over Easter, so he wasn't entitled to claim. You ever bloody heard anything like that?

ROSIE Oh, dear.

TOMMY I mean, I bet you an undercover Arab working over here – and there's plenty of 'em doing that – he'll be claiming for – whaddyacallit? – Ramadam, won't he? No, bloody '5, you forget them, darling.

ROSIE Right.

TOMMY You don't want to go joining them.

ROSIE I won't.

A pause. Tommy jiggles around restlessly again.

TOMMY Fancy one, do you? . . .

ROSIE No, thank you.

TOMMY Quick one? Only take five minutes?

ROSIE No, not at all.

TOMMY [*Unoffended*] Suit yourself. Just that some girls do. Some of the girls, they go barmy for –

ROSIE Listen, do you think I could just have a moment's quiet, please? To myself?

TOMMY Why's that?

ROSIE I need to get into character.

TOMMY [*Mystified by this*] What's that, then?

ROSIE If I'm to do this job properly, you see, I need a moment to concentrate on being Joanna Rupelford. That's all.

TOMMY Oh, right. Never heard of that before. Most of the girls, they just –

ROSIE Yes, well, I'm an exception.

TOMMY Right. Suit yourself, then . . . *Pause. [consulting his watch]* She's late, isn't she?

ROSIE [*Not being drawn*] Uh-huh.

TOMMY I can go down to a depth of one mile wearing this watch.

ROSIE I wish you would.

TOMMY Useful. [*Tommy now produces a short cosh-like implement from his belt. He thwacks it against his palm a few times*] Know what this is, then?

ROSIE Haven't the foggiest.

TOMMY It's known as a CQT. Close-quarters truncheon. Cutie for short. Special issue. [*He hits his palm again*] This could bring you to your knees, like that. Put you out for a month. Want to feel it? Go on. Have a feel of that.

ROSIE I don't want to feel it, thank you.

TOMMY Really. Some girls, they love to –

ROSIE Will you please shut up!

TOMMY Right. Suit yourself.

A silence. Tommy brandishes the truncheon a few more times.
I'll tell you one more thing, though –

ROSIE [*Thoroughly exasperated*] Oh, dear God!

TOMMY No, no. just one other thing. Even if you had this in your hand, even armed with this, you would never get within a yard of me. Do you know why that is?

ROSIE No, I can't imagine.

TOMMY Reflexes. I have incredible reflexes. They filmed me with the fastest film they had and they still couldn't catch the speed of my hands. True. When I was down there in Hereford, the instructor there told me I was seriously frightening.

ROSIE I know how he felt.

TOMMY Come on, you have a try. Come on. Have a try.

ROSIe No.

TOMMY Come on.

ROSIE No!

TOMMY Come on, it'll make you feel better. You see how fast I move, it'll make you feel better. Take it, go on, take it. [*He thrusts the cosh into Rosie's reluctant hand*]

ROSIE Oh, God.

TOMMY That's it, that's it! Now you come at me. Tell you what, I'll be behind the bar here, an innocent barman, you know. And you're coming in to rob me. Pretend you're trying to rob me. Come on then, girl. Now you come at me with the cosh, come and try hit me with it. And what I'll do, you see, is block it with one hand and at the same time disarm you with the other one. Now don't get nervous, I won't hurt you. Just try and hit me. Hit me with it, hard as you like. And you'll be amaze –

Rosie hits Tommy on the head. He is unprepared.

ROSIE [*Instantly appalled at what she's done*] Oh, God! I'm so sorry, I didn't mean to . . .

Tommy sways and his knees buckle.

TOMMY [*Feebly*] No, no. You got to wait till I'm ready, you see. Wait till I'm . . . [*He collapses*]

DRISCOLL   DORA
early 30s   late 20s
Irish

Haunting Dora
Jean Marlow
Eamonn Jones

First performed at the Theatre Royal, Margate in 2002, and set in
1928 when the variety theatre was being taken over by the 'Silver
Screen' and young, ambitious artistes were looking towards
Hollywood to further their careers.

DRISCOLL is an Irish comic – charming and whimsical, but with
one fatal flaw: he is always late. Late home, late for appointments,
even late on stage. Hoping to hit the big-time in films, he leaves
behind his beloved DORA and sets out for America. He takes a job as
a stuntman on a Tarzan picture, with disastrous results . . . True to
form he's late for his own funeral and is stuck in limbo.

Being a resourceful sort of 'spirit' he decides to visit his 'old
haunts' and finds himself back in an English seaside resort watching
a variety act at the local theatre. His old friends, Clara and Cyril are
on stage with the Magical Illusion act they have been performing for
the last 20 years. And the delightful DORA DEVINE is now a solo
artiste. Maybe he can get back with them again – if only he can find
a way . . .

DRISCOLL has persuaded his friends to let him stay with them that
night. Over a fish and chip supper he regales them with exaggerated
tales of his Hollywood exploits. Long after Clara and DORA have
retired to bed, he and Cyril are sharing a bottle of scotch together
and talking about old times.

In this scene it is early next morning. DRISCOLL is still sitting in
the armchair he occupied the previous night with a second bottle of
scotch in front of him. He quickly drains his glass and pours himself
another as DORA enters.

Available from Brian Schwartz, Offstage Bookshop, London

DORA Oh, good morning, Driscoll.

DRISCOLL Mornin', Dora.

DORA Cyril's still in bed. You must have had quite a night the pair of you.

DRISCOLL You can say that again!

DORA Doesn't seem to have affected you much. I expect you were talking about old times.

DRISCOLL Yes, old times . . .

DORA Fancy being in all those films and me not knowing about it.

DRISCOLL They haven't been shown over here yet.

DORA Ramon Novarraa, Pola Negri, Myrna Loy – Oh, I think she's lovely! And Bessie Love . . . to think I was watching her in *Broadway Melody* only last week, and you've actually spoken to her . . . Worked with her. It's wonderful Driscoll, simply wonderful!

DRISCOLL I suppose so, yes. But you take it all for granted after a while.

DORA I wouldn't. I wouldn't take it for granted. Not ever, I wouldn't. Oh, Driscoll, I wish I could have been with you.

DRISCOLL So do I, Dora. So do I.

DORA [*shyly*] I missed you so much, Driscoll. You'll never know how much I missed you.

DRISCOLL Me too, Dora. I missed you too.

DORA But I never gave up hope . . . Like Lilian Gish in *The White Sister* I kept my little flame burning. Oh, I realise now, you had to go.

DRISCOLL [*playing the game*] That's right, I did, I did. I was no good to you, Dora. I had no money and nothing to offer you. You didn't deserve it, being stuck with a no good second rater like I was then. I had to go forward, move on. I know I must have hurt you. But I always meant to come back. As soon as I'd made my fame and fortune, I always meant to come back.

DORA [*Won over*] Like Ramon Navarro in *The Return*?

DRISCOLL Something like that, yes.

DORA Oh I think it's so thrilling, really thrilling. When they show your films over here, people will be queuing up for your autograph. You'll have to go out in disguise. You know, wearing dark glasses like Douglas Fairbanks . . .

DRISCOLL [*modestly*] I don't know about that.

DORA You could be mobbed . . . [*thinks*] We could be mobbed . . .

DRISCOLL We?

DORA Well, if I was out with you, we'd be mobbed together, wouldn't we? I can see it all. Women fighting to get a glimpse of you. Children lifted up on high. Men trying to shake hands with you. And the police holding back the crowds, making a pathway for us to walk through.

DRISCOLL Steady on, old girl . . . When I was on the set of *Bulldog Drummond* we had an actress. Bennett was her name. Joan Bennett. I had this scene where I rescue her from the villain. Well just when I got to my most dramatic lines, 'Stand back you cad and take what's coming to you!' the studio cat walked across the set and she let out the most enormous scream . . .

Dora is staring at him.

DRISCOLL What's the matter?

DORA Did you say *Bulldog Drummond*?

DRISCOLL That's right, yes. As I was saying, she let out this enormous scream just as I was about to say my lines . . . I say, are you alright?

DORA **Your** lines.

DRISCOLL Yes . . . What is it, Dora? What's the matter?

DORA They were Ronald Coleman's lines. I've seen that film twenty-one times. I know it off by heart.

DRISCOLL It hasn't been shown here yet.

DORA Oh yes it has. It was on again last week.

Driscoll looks crestfallen and then recovers himself.

DRISCOLL Of course, how silly of me! What am I talking about. *Bulldog Drummond*! I meant *Big Boy*. That's it, *Big Boy*.

DORA That was Al Jolson.

An awkward pause.

DORA Driscoll. You haven't been telling me the truth, have you? Come on, own up. It was all stories, wasn't it? Like the ones you used to tell me when we were on tour.

DRISCOLL I thought you enjoyed my stories.

DORA I want the truth, Driscoll. [*She puts her hand on her heart in film-type gesture*] You owe me that at least.

DRISCOLL Well now, let me see . . . there's truth . . . and truth. It all depends on the sort of truth you're looking for.

DORA [*exasperated*] Oh Driscoll!

DRISCOLL Now there's the sort of truth that does nobody any good, what my old Granny called 'home truth', and then there's the sort of truth with a bit of fancy to it – a **much** better truth to my way of thinking – gives everybody a bit of pleasure and something to look forward to.

DORA [*tearful*] It's all very well for you . . .

DRISCOLL Now cheer up, old girl. There's no harm done. After all . . .

DORA You can stand there and say, 'No harm done!' You come back seven years late telling me a lot of stupid stories and making a fool of yourself in front of Cyril and Clara and then you say there's no harm done!

DRISCOLL You don't let me finish, Dora. That's always been your trouble. Too quick off the mark, if you don't mind my saying. Too ready to jump to conclusions. I **was** in Hollywood . . .

DORA Not in films, though.

DRISCOLL There you go again!

DORA How can I believe a word you . . .

DRISCOLL **And** I was in *Broadway Melody*. **And** I was in *The White Sister* . . .

DORA Driscoll, stop it!

DRISCOLL And *The Light Is Dark* and *Daredevil Jack*, *The Woman He Scorned*, *The Student Prince*, *Her Private Life*, *Lily of the Dust* and *Forbidden Paradise* and . . . and *Phantom of the Opera* . . .

DORA [*Hands over her ears and shutting her eyes*] Stop it! Stop it! I won't listen to any more!

DRISCOLL [*shouting*] But it happens to be **true**, Dora! All true!

Dora opens one eye.

DRISCOLL The only difference is . . . I didn't play opposite Bessie Love and Joan Bennett, that's all.

DORA Who did you play opposite, then?

DRISCOLL You really want to know?

DORA Yes.

DRISCOLL I didn't play opposite anyone . . .

There is a long pause while Dora looks at him, not knowing if this is another one of his stories.

DRISCOLL But I drove off the end of the pier, I escaped from a burning building, I leapt from an express train and rolled all the way down the embankment. I was a cowboy, a racing driver, an escaped gorilla and a sea monster. I climbed the belfry and swung on the bells . . .

DORA *Hunchback of Notre Dame!*

DRISCOLL And rode a white charger across the desert . . .

DORA [*clapping her hands*] *Son of the Sheik!*

DRISCOLL But I never got my name in lights . . . never even got a mention . . . [*pause*] I was a Stand-In, Dora . . . An Extra . . . Promise you won't tell Cyril and Clara.

DORA Not if you don't want me to. [*She sighs, then making the best of things*] But you know, Lon Chaney started out as an Extra and Ronald Coleman only walked across the set in *The Dauntless Three*. Perhaps you gave up too soon.

DRISCOLL I was getting tired of it all. It's a young man's game. Getting up at five every morning. And it wasn't much fun when Prohibition came in, you know. There was no drop of the hard stuff to steady the nerves . . . Mind you, there were ways and means of overcoming all that. I remember one of the last stunts I did. It was a freezing cold morning – it often is in California – and there I was, up at five as usual. I'd drunk half a bottle of scotch before they put me on my horse . . . they actually had to tie me on, you know. Then the Props Man gave the horse a slap on the rump and off we galloped . . . I had this lasso, you see. And I had to throw it over the runaway horse in front of me. Ah, he was a wild one. I whirled the lasso three times around my head – whoosh, whoosh, whoosh – and then let it go . . . It snaked out towards the stallion – a beautiful sight to see – and then . . . and then . . .

DORA What happened then? Go with the story. What happened, Driscoll?

DRISCOLL Funny thing, I don't remember . . . I simply don't remember . . . except that I woke up in hospital with a broken leg and two broken arms and you see that mark there . . .

DORA I think so, Driscoll.

DRISCOLL Twenty-five stitches . . . And me back – me back'll never be the same . . .

DORA Oh, Driscoll . . .

CECILY CARDEW   ALGERNON MONCRIEFF
young   young

The Importance of Being Earnest
Oscar Wilde

This comedy of manners was first performed at St James's Theatre,
London in 1895.

At the beginning of the play ALGERNON's friend, Jack Worthing,
explains that he always assumes the name of a mythical younger
brother, 'Ernest', when he is in town, in order to excuse his frequent
absences from his country home. Jack's young ward, CECILY is
intrigued by this mythical younger brother and when she eventually
meets ALGERNON, who pretends be 'Ernest' in order to gain
admittance to Jack's country home, she immediately falls in love with
him.

In this earlier scene CECILY is sitting in the garden studying her
German lesson, when the butler brings her a card, announcing the
arrival of 'Mr Ernest Worthing'. She is thrilled to be meeting her
Uncle Jack's wicked younger brother at last.

Published by *New Mermaids*, A & C Black, London

CECILY [*takes the card and reads it*] "Mr Ernest Worthing, B.4, The
Albany, W." Uncle Jack's brother! . . . I have never met any really
wicked person before. I feel rather frightened. I am so afraid he
will look just like everyone else.
Enter Algernon, very gay and debonair.
He does!
ALGERNON [*raising hat*] You are my little cousin Cecily, I'm sure.
CECILY You are under some strange mistake. I am not little. In fact,
I believe I am more than usually tall for my age. [*Algernon is
rather taken aback*] But I am your cousin Cecily. You, I see from
your card, are Uncle Jack's brother, my cousin Ernest, my wicked
cousin Ernest.

ALGERNON Oh! I am not really wicked at all, cousin Cecily. You musn't think that I am wicked.

CECILY If you are not, then you have certainly been deceiving us all in a very inexcusable manner. You have made Uncle Jack believe that you are very bad. I hope you have not been leading a double life, pretending to be wicked and being really good all the time. That would be hypocrisy.

ALGERNON [*looks at her in amazement*] Oh! Of course I have been rather reckless.

CECILY I am glad to hear it.

ALGERNON In fact, now you mention the subject, I have been very bad in my own small way.

CECILY I don't think you should be so proud of that, though I am sure it must have been very pleasant.

ALGERNON It is much pleasanter being here with you.

CECILY I can't understand how you are here at all. Uncle Jack telegraphed to you yesterday at the Albany that he would see you for the last time at six o'clock. He lets me read all the telegrams he sends you. I know some of them by heart.

ALGERNON The fact is I didn't get the telegram till it was too late. Then I missed him at the Club, and the Hall Porter said he thought he had come down here. So, of course, I followed as I knew he wanted to see me.

CECILY He won't be back till Monday afternoon.

ALGERNON That is a great disappointment. I am obliged to go up by the first train on Monday morning. I have a business appointment that I am anxious . . . to miss!

CECILY Couldn't you miss it anywhere but in London?

ALGERNON No: the appointment is in London.

CECILY Well, I know, of course, how important it is not to keep a business engagement, if one wants to retain any sense of the beauty of life, but still I think you had better wait till Uncle Jack arrives. I know he wants to speak to you about your emigrating.

ALGERNON About my what?

CECILY Your emigrating. He has gone up to buy your outfit.

ALGERNON I certainly wouldn't let Jack buy my outfit. He has no taste in neckties at all.

CECILY I don't think you will require neckties. Uncle Jack is sending you to Australia.

ALGERNON Australia! I'd sooner die.

CECILY Well, he said at dinner on Wednesday night, that you would have to choose between this world, the next world, and Australia.

ALGERNON Oh, well! The accounts I have received of Australia and the next world, are not particularly encouraging. This world is good enough for me, cousin Cecily.

CECILY Yes, but are you good enough for it?

ALGERNON I'm afraid I'm not that. That is why I want you to reform me. You might make that your mission, if you don't mind, cousin Cecily.

CECILY How dare you suggest that I have a mission?

ALGERNON I beg your pardon: but I thought that every woman had a mission of some kind, nowadays.

CECILY Every female has! No woman. Besides, I have no time to reform you this afternoon.

ALGERNON Well, would you mind my reforming myself this afternoon?

CECILY It is rather Quixotic of you. But I think you should try.

ALGERNON I will. I feel better already.

CECILY You are looking a little worse.

ALGERNON That is because I am hungry.

CECILY How thoughtless of me. I should have remembered that when one is going to lead an entirely new life, one requires regular and wholesome meals. Miss Prism and I lunch at two, off some roast mutton.

ALGERNON I fear that would be too rich for me.

CECILY Uncle Jack, whose health has been sadly undermined by the late hours you keep in town, has been ordered by his London doctor to have pâté de foie gras sandwiches and 1889 champagne at twelve. I don't know if such invalid fare would suit you.

ALGERNON Oh! I will be quite content with '89 champagne.

CECILY I am glad to see you have such simple tastes. This is the dining-room.

ALGERNON Thank you. Might I have a buttonhole first? I never have any appetite unless I have a buttonhole first.

CECILY A Maréchal Niel? [*Picks up scissors*]

ALGERNON No, I'd sooner have a pink rose.

CECILY Why? [*Cuts a flower*]

ALGERNON Because you are like a pink rose, Cousin Cecily.

CECILY I don't think it can be right for you to talk to me like that. Miss Prism never says such things to me.

ALGERNON Then Miss Prism is a short-sighted old lady. [*Cecily puts the rose in his buttonhole*] You are the prettiest girl I ever saw.

CECILY Miss Prism says that all good looks are a snare.

ALGERNON They are a snare that every sensible man would like to be caught in.

CECILY Oh, I don't think I would care to catch a sensible man. I shouldn't know what to talk to him about.

They pass into the house.

PEG WOFFINGTON
early 30s
Irish

DAVID GARRICK
30s

A Laughing Matter
April De Angelis

First produced by Out of Joint and the Royal National Theatre at the Yvonne Arnaud Theatre, Guildford in October 2002. It was then transferred to the National in November in repertoire with Oliver Goldsmith's *She Stoops To Conquer* and returned there in February 2003.

A Laughing Matter is set in 18th century London and is described as 'an irreverent version of real-life events'. It tells the story of actor manager David Garrick, Dr Johnson, Oliver Goldsmith and a new play, *She Stoops To Conquer*, written by Goldsmith. Caught up between financial pressures and artistic ambition, GARRICK must make up his mind whether to risk staging a play that could make or break his career.

GARRICK has just taken over as Manager at Drury Lane and is introducing a new repertoire of plays into his forthcoming season.

In this scene GARRICK is alone, rehearsing with a retractable knife. He is confronted by PEG WOFFINGTON – his ex-mistress and leading lady, famous for her breeches part of Sir Harry Wildair in Farquhar's *Constant Couple*.

Published by Faber & Faber, London

GARRICK By the immortal destiny that dooms
   Me to this cursed minute
   I'll not live one longer.
Peg Woffington enters.
GARRICK It's not for personal use, you understand.
WOFFINGTON I'm here because you want to destroy me.
GARRICK Don't go all dramatic on me.
WOFFINGTON To take away my work.
GARRICK That is a typical Woffington overreaction.

WOFFINGTON That is a typical Garrick obfuscation.

GARRICK It's standard practice for a new manager to create a new repertoire.

WOFFINGTON With none of my parts in it.

GARRICK We will, of course, be looking at new ways of including you in the season. This isn't personal.

WOFFINGTON You still love me and out of sheer bitterness you want to destroy me.

GARRICK Peg, I'm about to be a happily married man.

WOFFINGTON I've met a lot of those.

GARRICK I know. I made a list of all your misdemeanours. I found it the other day and had a good laugh.

WOFFINGTON I suppose you were clearing things out.

GARRICK My wife and I will be moving into our new home.

WOFFINGTON You're not clearing me out of the theatre. Why have you cut *The Constant Couple*? Nobody does Sir Harry like I do. I've got the legs for it. [*She shows her legs*]

GARRICK Put those away.

WOFFINGTON They're only legs. Nothing to be scared of. You've seem them before.

GARRICK If Sir Harry Wildair gets done again, he won't be played by a woman.

WOFFINGTON Why not? I made that part.

GARRICK It is now considered vulgar for a woman to play a man.

WOFFINGTON Don't be a prick.

GARRICK Unfortunately there are a lot of pricks that think the same way and they buy the tickets.

WOFFINGTON So what if I show my legs? Theatre isn't church. If it was, people would stop going.

GARRICK Your theatre is finished. People are eager for change and I want to give it to them. Emotion, not cynicism. Dignity, not immorality.

WOFFINGTON I bet you never fucked her yet, have you?

GARRICK No, because she's been well brought up.

WOFFINGTON I'd rather come from the gutter than from genteel poverty like you, forever sewing pockets over holes. I'd rather go naked.

GARRICK Which you do with great frequency.

WOFFINGTON I don't know why God gave you your talent, because it's wasted on you. Always bowing and scraping and scared of what you want.

GARRICK I got what I wanted.

WOFFINGTON Bastard. [*She picks up a knife*]

GARRICK That's retractable.

WOFFINGTON Typical. When I chose you, you ran off. That's what I don't understand – how you started out brave and ended up a coward.

GARRICK After two years of putting up with you and your numerous infidelities, are you suggesting I should have stayed?

WOFFINGTON My lovers gave you an excuse. You wanted this theatre, not me.

GARRICK Yes, I was tired of your world and its casual humiliations. It was cruel.

WOFFINGTON I'll go to Dublin; the management there has a bit of sense. My life from now on doesn't look so bad: twenty-seven, beautiful, the toast of the Dublin stage. Yours looks a lot worse: married to a virgin and arse-licking your way around London.

GARRICK Mrs Woffington is leaving us, Susannah. [*to Peg*] May I offer you the usual sentiments?

WOFFINGTON Shove your sentiments.

MRS TULL   MARTIN
middle-aged   young

Mother Clap's Molly House
Mark Ravenhill

First performed at the Lyttelton Theatre, Royal National Theatre in 2001 and set in the London of 1726 and in present time.

When MRS TULL's husband dies she is left alone with only MARTIN, the apprentice boy, to help her run their tally shop, and hire out costumes to the local whores.

A Wake is held in the tally shop, where Stephen Tull's body lies in its open coffin. Friends and neighbours, and among them the whores, are calling out for MRS TULL but she has taken to her bed, too tired and upset to join them. MARTIN sends everyone away and MRS TULL appears. She tells MARTIN she will be closing down the tally shop. She cannot afford new stock and has never learnt to keep a ledger. MARTIN will have to find himself a new place.

At the beginning of this scene she is alone with Stephen Tull's body. As she begs him to tell her what she should do, MARTIN returns, carrying a large bundle of very grand dresses.

Note: Mother Clap's Molly House was developed with students from the London Academy of Music and Dramatic Arts. In this extract, an oblique (/) denotes interrupted speech.

Published by Methuen, London

MARTIN Look! Look! Look!

TULL What you got there, Martin?

MARTIN New stock. Look. [*He opens the bundle and pulls out some very grand dresses*] In't that wonderful? See? In't that something'll fetch a good price? And here. Now – you ever seen fairer than that?

TULL Where it all come from?

MARTIN Business'll take a turn with this, wun't it? Once word is out, we got this in stock, there'll be customers crowding in morning and night.

TULL Where you get it?

MARTIN It's what he would want. Business got to go on.

TULL They stolen goods?

MARTIN Dun't matter.

TULL Thought so. Martin. Thass wrong. Stolen goods.

MARTIN But that's business.

TULL Not this business.

MARTIN *sighs*

TULL Or you'll swing, boy. That what you want?

MARTIN *shrugs*

TULL Well, I'll make sure you do. Because I'll go to the constables myself, see?

MARTIN No you / bloody well won't.

TULL I shall. I love a hanging. I'll follow that cart through the streets and every rattle of the wheels I'll be calling: 'I told you so, I told you so.' Last thing you see as your neck goes crack will be me with a 'Didn't I say so?' on my lips. And there won't be no ballads or stories about you. Boy who stole dresses. Nobody'll remember that.

MARTIN You reckon? Then you do without me, see? You get by on / your own.

TULL Oh, I shall / I shall. I'll do that.

MARTIN You see how long you keep / going without me.

TULL You go back on the streets. You live like an animal. Go on. GO ON. [*Pause*] Well, there's a fair old row, in't there?

MARTIN You got a big old mouth on you.

TULL Big as yours. Don't want to see you hang. Want you to take care of yourself, see? Because . . .

MARTIN Because . . . ? [*Pause*] You gonna write it in the book? Thass what Master always did.

TULL I don't know how.

MARTIN You'll work it out. Here.

Martin gives Tull the ledger.

TULL Can't work it out.

MARTIN Mrs Tull, you gotta . . . I'm looking to you. I in't Man, I'm Boy. Boy needs protecting, guiding, boy needs . . . Look after me. Thass your duty.

TULL Love, I in't up to that. I'm frightened.

MARTIN You wanna little beer, calm yourself?

TULL Well, maybe I should.

Martin goes to pour Tull a beer.

MARTIN None left. They must have been awful drinkers.

TULL Right enough. More drinking than mourning I should say.

MARTIN I could run and fetch you some beer.

TULL Yes. A little more beer and then to bed. Here. [*She gives Martin a coin from her purse*] Just mind you come straight back. You're an awful wanderer.

MARTIN Don't mean to be.

TULL I'd say to him: Oh, that boy's an awful wanderer. One day he'll wander off the edge of the world and they'll be no one there to catch him. Where do you go, Martin, when you're a-wandering?

MARTIN Nowhere.

TULL Take a lot of time going nowhere.

MARTIN Nowhere special.

TULL Well – jug of beer and then straight back. Thass straight back.

MARTIN Voice big as that, you could run a tally shop.

TULL You reckon?

MARTIN Oh yeah. You can be Master now.

TULL [*laughs*] Don't know about that.

Exit Martin.

TULL [*goes over to the stolen dresses. Picks one up*] Well, in't that . . . Very fine. [*Another dress*] Ooo, this'd fetch a good price. [*Another dress*] Needs work but . . . [*Looks at ledger*] Well and maybe I could . . . [*Searches through ledger*] Goods in, goods in. Goods in! [*Writes down first item*] Well and that in't a bad hand. Come on then, girl. Write 'em.

LADY ONOLA
30s–40s
African

OROMBO
30s–40s
African

Oroonoko

Aphra Behn
Adaptation by 'Biyi Bandele

This new adaptation of Aphra Behn's novella was first performed by the Royal Shakespeare Company at the Other Place, Stratford-upon-Avon in 1999.

It tells the story of a young African Prince, Oroonoko, who is tricked into slavery and transported to Surinam in South America where he is persuaded to lead a slave revolt.

In this scene, set in the King's palace in Coramantien, Oroonoko asks for an audience with the King, his Grandfather, but OROMBO, the King's Chief Advisor tells him that His Highness is 'attending to eminently urgent affairs of state'. At that moment LADY ONOLA, a middle-aged courtesan enters. She is the outspoken ex-mistress of the King and is allowed to remain at court as she is the one person who is not afraid to tell His Highness – or anyone else – the truth.

Published by Amber Lane Press, Oxford

ONOLA Affairs of the state? Did you say
    Affairs of the state?
    [*to Oroonoko*] What Chief Orombo means is that His
    Highness our dear King is keeping
    His visitors waiting while he attempts
    To insert his Royal Privilege
    Into the comely virtues of a young maiden.
    Much ado – dare I say – over nothing.
    Were the King's penis a warrior – he
    Wishes it were – it would have been beheaded
    Long ago for persistent dereliction of duty . . .
    It is well known in the seraglio

That though the King never can
Sleep, his penis is forever nodding off.
OROMBO [*indignantly*] Two of my own wives have had the rare
Privilege of supping with the King. And
Upon their word – they have no reason to lie –
ONOLA – They do lie – with every boy-slave in the land.
OROMBO [*chokes*] – Upon their word, the Royal Manhood is as
Long as the Royal Python.
ONOLA Your wives may have slept with a snake,
Chief Orombo, but not with the one
Between the King's legs. It is a worm
Bereft of limb, flattered into thinking
Itself a reptile.
OROMBO How dare you, Lady Onola!
How dare you!
ONOLA I did tell your second wife, Kemi, when she said
She was marrying you that you had not
Done badly by her, for she is beautiful and
So is her smile. You bedecked her with gold and bales
Of cloth. But I could see, from looking at you,
That you could not satisfy her in bed. What
She needed in bed – I told her – was a man who once he
Mounted her would not let off until the roof fell
Through. Not a glorified pimp who farms out
His wives and children to curry royal favour.
OROMBO [*stiffly*] It's called loyalty, Lady Onola, which
Comes from Good Breeding. Have you
Heard of Good Breeding? Ah, there I go again.
Forgive me. Just like me to forget that you
Were bred in a bordello.
In any case I don't see how what I do or choose not to
Do with my family is any of your business. And we are
Talking not about me but about the Royal Manhood.
Help me out, Praise-Singers!

RITA	PHIL
20s	20s
Welsh	Welsh

A Prayer for Wings
Sean Mathias

First presented at the Edinburgh Festival at the Scottish Centre in 1985 and later transferred to the Bush Theatre, London.

The action takes place in an old church that has been poorly converted into a dwelling on the outskirts of Swansea, where RITA lives with her invalid mother. Every day she has to wash, dress, shop, cook for her and help her out of her wheelchair. Unemployment is high and she can't get a job. Her only break in the monotony is touching up the boys down at the Labour for a few shillings and sometimes bringing them back to her upstairs bedroom to earn a bit more. She prays for a 'handsome man with real manners'. If she had wings she could fly away.

In this scene her prayer is about to be answered.

Published by Amber Lane Press, Oxford

RITA Come in, Phil. But be quiet, mind. My Mam is sleeping. This way. Follow me. This way. [*Rita leads Phil to her bedroom*] There. This is my room.

PHIL Very nice, Beautiful home.

RITA D'you think?

PHIL Yes. Unusual.

RITA It's certainly that.

PHIL Strange, living in a church, mind.

RITA It's certainly that. Still, it suits us.

PHIL Well, that's what counts, innit?

RITA So you've just moved in?

PHIL Yes. Moved down the other end of the terrace. [*Pause*] You got lovely hair.

RITA Oh, get on.

PHIL No 'tis, mind. Lovely. Beautiful colour.

RITA Thank you.

PHIL 'tis, mind.

RITA Where d'you say you come from?

PHIL Port Talbot.

RITA We comes from Neath. My Aunty lived down this terrace. Died down this terrace.

PHIL My Dad's got a job in Swansea. Down the M.O.T. Centre. That's why we're here. He's lucky to get a job these days, mind. [*Pause*] Can I touch your hair?

RITA Course.

[*Phil touches Rita's hair*]

[*aside*] There's a lovely manner on him. And he've got the face of an angel. Beautiful complexion.

PHIL You got lovely hair.

RITA [*aside*] This one's a real gent. Phil. It's a handsome name. He's a handsome boy. Handsome face. A face that would turn your eyes to tears. Make your heart swell. Yes Boy, I'll have you.

[*Rita smiles at Phil. A pause*]

PHIL D'you think I could kiss you?

RITA Course.

[*They kiss, then break away*]

[*aside*] Oh, God, I was never expecting you to send no angel from Port Talbot. He's a gem of a kisser.

PHIL Where's your Mam?

RITA She's sleeping. Having her kip. She's a cripple. [*Phil is genuinely surprised*]

PHIL Oh!

RITA Didn't them boys tell you?

PHIL What boys?

RITA That snotty lot on the corner.

PHIL I never spoke to them.

RITA Get on! Then how come you was down the Reck?

PHIL Just having a walk. Why? Mind, I was pleased when you come up to me, 'cos I never spoke to no-one round here. Why?

RITA [*aside*] Oh! A real gent. He's a shy boy. Not the sort to go interfering. To have and to hold. [*to Phil*] Oh, nothing. Wanna kiss me again?

PHIL [*grinning*] Course.

[*They kiss, then break away*]

RITA [*aside*] Aye, there's a kiss. A kiss that'd banish the devil from this church. [*to Phil*] So, you got no friends round here?

PHIL No, none. [*Pause*] Only you.

RITA [*aside*] Oh, he knows the direct line to a girl's heart. [*to Phil*] Yeah. We'll be friends, Phil. You'll always be welcome in our house.

PHIL I'd like that. I'd be glad to be your friend. Maybe we could go to the pictures?

RITA [*aside*] He's everything I've ever dreamt of. His hands, his hair, his speech, his corduroys. We'll go out dancing. And make love at midnight. [*to Phil*] Oh, yes, I love the pictures.

PHIL We'll go into town. To one of them Complex Cinemas.

RITA Only thing is, we can't see a long film 'cos of my Mam.

PHIL I'd like to meet her.

RITA You could come for tea. Meet Mam. She'd be intrigued to meet you. Mind you, she've got a funny attitude towards blokes. [*aside*] But then this one's no ordinary bloke.

PHIL You got a lovely face, Reet. A really lovely face.

RITA Go on. No-one ever said that before [*aside*] 'cept Mam. [*to Phil*] Except my Mam.

PHIL Well, you have, Reet.

RITA And no-one ever called me that before. Except my Mam.

PHIL Sorry. D'you mind?

RITA No. Call me what you like, Boy.

PHIL Here then, Reet, can I ask you a question?

RITA Fire away.

PHIL Will you go out with me?

RITA Aye. I've said I'll go to the pictures with you.

PHIL I don't mean that. Not just that. I mean out . . . out.

[*Pause*]

RITA You mean like stepping out?

PHIL Yeah. That's right. Like that. Will you, Rita? Will you?

RITA [*aside*] Yes, Boy, I'll have you, to have and to hold, from this day forth, sickness – God help – and health, richer – please God – or poorer. And I'll give you four bouncing boys. Little captains they'll be. And we'll travel. Travel across continents. And have a lovely house.

PHIL Will you, Reet? Will you?

RITA Yes, Phil. I will. I'll go out with you. Anywhere you suggests. Everywhere you takes me.

PHIL You got lovely hair, Rita. Really lovely. [*Phil touches Rita's hair again*] Here. How about another kiss?

RITA [*aside*] Sealed with a loving kiss. [*to Phil*] Course.

[*They kiss, then break away*]

And you must come back and meet my Mam. We'll have tea together. You're always welcome here, mind, Phil.

PHIL Thanks, Rita. I think you're smashing. [*Pause*] I'd best be off, then.

RITA Go on, then, Phil. You go now. Call tomorrow, 'bout four o'clock. We'll go for a walk.

PHIL Aye, all right, Rita. I'll see you tomorrow, then.

RITA All right, Phil. [*Phil starts to go*] Here, and Phil.

PHIL Yes, Rita?

RITA Welcome to the terrace.

PHIL Thank you, Rita. I feels it. Most welcome. Not like Port Talbot down here, it isn't. Not like Port Talbot at all.

[*Phil goes out the front door, shutting it gently behind him*]

JEAN BRODIE
early middle-age
Edinburgh Scots

GORDON LOWTHER
youngish
Edinburgh Scots

The Prime of Miss Jean Brodie
Jay Presson Allen
Adapted from the novel by Muriel Spark

First presented at the Wyndhams Theatre, London in 1966 and at the Helen Hayes Theater, New York in 1968.

JEAN BRODIE, a spinster whose fiancé was killed in World War I, is an English teacher at the Marcia Blaine Academy. Many of her colleagues disapprove of her unconventional teaching methods, but she is popular among the girls, particularly her special students who become known as the 'Brodie Set'. She becomes involved with art teacher, Teddy Lloyd and later the new music teacher, GORDON LOWTHER. Out of patience with the situation and unable to tolerate the increasing rumours about MISS BRODIE, the Headmistress, Miss Mackay – in the presence of GORDON LOWTHER – demands her resignation.

In this scene, JEAN BRODIE strides nervily across her classroom to clean a blackboard that doesn't need cleaning. The door opens and GORDON LOWTHER enters, carrying his golf clubs from the previous scene.

Published by Samuel French Inc., New York

LOWTHER Oh, Jean! You were wonderful. Miss Mackay wants to make it up!

BRODIE [*Grimly triumphant*] I'm sure she does!

LOWTHER You were heroic! Heroic! It was inspiring! Oh, if only I could have stood up like that to Mr Gaunt! If I could have said, 'Mr Gaunt! If you have one authentic shred of evidence – just one – '

BRODIE What are you talking about?

LOWTHER Mr Gaunt called on me the night before last. He advised me to resign as organist and elder of the church. He spoke very plainly.

BRODIE [*Militantly*] And what did you answer?

LOWTHER [*Helplessly*] He left me no alternative, Jean. I – resigned.

BRODIE You *allowed* this evil-minded man – a man who uses his position as minister of the gospel to encourage the slanderous gossip of petty provincials –

LOWTHER But Jean! It isn't just gossip! You do not go home on Sunday nights!

BRODIE They have no proof! Can't you see that resignation is tantamount to a confession of guilt?

LOWTHER [*With great feeling*] I *feel* guilty!

BRODIE Well, *I* do *not!*

LOWTHER [*Sinks into one of the student's chairs, drained, utterly fatigued*] Oh, Jean . . . it's been going on so long. Can't you see, I am not cut out to be a – [*Ducks his head, whispers*] a philanderer!

BRODIE [*Throws back her head and laughs*] A philanderer! Oh, Gordon!

LOWTHER [*Stubbornly*] Will you not marry me at last and put an end to all this sneaking about?

BRODIE [*Laughs*] Only today I was told to my face that you plan to marry the Chemistry teacher.

LOWTHER [*Abashed*] I played golf with Miss Lockhart once.

BRODIE Twice.

LOWTHER [*A paroxysm of shame*] Twice.

BRODIE Beware. Don't trifle with her. [*She points a gun-like finger at his temple*] She has the means to blow us all up.

LOWTHER Jean . . . Miss Lockhart means nothing to me. You know that. It's just that so much of the time now you are busy.

BRODIE If you would only be persuaded to take a flat in Edinburgh –

LOWTHER I do not *want* a flat in Edinburgh. Cramond is my home! I was born there! You know I could not leave Cramond. I don't *want* to leave Cramond.

BRODIE You want a great deal, do you not?

LOWTHER [*Contritely*] What I want mostly, Jean, is to see you happy and *safe*.

BRODIE Safe? And what, pray, does safety have to do with happiness? [*Laughs*] I am not an admirer of Stanley Baldwin. [*Suddenly fidgety and agitated*] Oh, do run along, Gordon. My class is almost due and I need to compose myself.

LOWTHER I don't understand you. You will not marry me and yet you feed me and share my bed.

BRODIE Share your bed. Why can't you say you are my lover?

LOWTHER I do not *want* to be your lover! I want to be your husband! And I'm sick and tired of all that rich, undomestic food. I want to go on my honeymoon to the Isle of Eigg near Rum where my mother and father went on their honeymoon, and I want to come back to Cramond with my bride! *That's* what I want! [*He stomps to the door then turns*] And I wanted to conduct the church choir, too! [*He is gone*]

ARNOLPHE
middle-aged

AGNES
young

The School for Wives
Molière
Translated by Maya Slater

First produced in Paris in the original as *L'Ecole des Femmes* at the Palais-Royal in 1662, this latest translation was published in 2001.

ARNOLPHE, anxious to find a wife who will never be unfaithful to him, selects his ward, AGNES, an innocent young girl who has been brought up in a convent, as his future bride. But AGNES meets and falls in love with Horace, a young man whose father is ARNOLPHE's friend.

In this scene ARNOLPHE has just discovered that an unknown man has been seen visiting his ward and has bribed the servants, Georgette and Alain to let him into the house. He is eaten up with misery and rage, but is determined to control himself. He invites AGNES to go for a walk with him so that he can talk to her alone.

From *The Misanthrope, Tartuffe and Other Plays* in the Oxford World's Classics series, published by Oxford University Press

Act Two, Scene Five
ARNOLPHE A fine day for a walk.
AGNES Yes, fine.
ARNOLPHE Fine weather, too
AGNES Yes, fine.
ARNOLPHE What's new? Let's talk . . .
    You know, Agnes, my dear, the world's a funny place.
    There's so much idle gossip, it's quite hard to face.
    Some neighbours told me that a young man no one knew
    Came to the house when I was gone, just to see you,
    And you let him come in, and even socialize –
    But I told them their tattle was a pack of lies,
    And I was keen to bet they'd made a bad mistake . . .

AGNES Oh, goodness, please don't bet, because you'll lose your
  stake!
ARNOLPHE What! So it really happened, and this man . . .
AGNES It's true! He hardly left the house for days, I promise you!
ARNOLPHE [*aside*] At least she's quite sincere, and since she has
  confessed,
  It's clear her innocence at least has stood the test. [*Aloud*]
  But if I'm not mistaken, surely I recall
  I said to turn away all strangers who might call.
AGNES Yes, but you don't know how it happened, do you see.
  I tell you, you'd have acted just the same as me.
ARNOLPHE Perhaps; but meanwhile, tell me how it came about.
AGNES It's quite amazing, very odd as you'll find out:
  As I was sitting sewing on the balcony,
  I raised my eyes and saw, beneath that very tree,
  A handsome, fine young man, who, seeing me up there,
  Bowed most respectfully, and with a courtly air.
  I wanted to be civil, that was my concern,
  So I made a respectful curtsey, in my turn.
  He bowed again most promptly, not to be outdone,
  And I produced a curtsey. Well, we'd just begun . . .
  And if the evening hadn't come, I'm telling you,
  I would have gone on standing there, till now. It's true –
  I'd never once have given in, it couldn't be
  That he should think me less polite and nice than he.
ARNOLPHE That's good!
AGNES As I was standing by the door next day,
  An old woman came up, and spoke to me this way:
  'My child, may the good Lord protect you, and preserve
  Those lovely looks for many a long year. I observe
  That God made you a pretty girl; but he did not
  Intend you to misuse the gifts that you have got:
  For you must know that you have practically slain
  A heart, and forced a man to cry aloud in pain.'
ARNOLPHE [*aside*] You devilish old hag, I hate you, damn your eyes!
AGNES She told me: 'What he needs to stop him getting worse,
  Is just to sit with you a little, and converse . . .
  'I willingly agree,' said I. 'If that's the case,
  He's welcome to come round and see me at our place.'
ARNOLPHE [*aside*] You execrable witch, you got me in this fix!
  May hell repay you for your charitable tricks!

AGNES Now you know why he came to see me in his plight.
I cured him. Don't you think, yourself, that I did right? . . .
He brought a most delightful casket which he set
Before me, and gave cash to Alain and Georgette.
You'd have been just as pleased as us, if you had known . . .
ARNOLPHE Yes, but what did he do, when you two were alone?
AGNES He swore his love for me was endless; in a word,
He said the sweetest things that you have ever heard.
I've never listened to such words as that before.
And when I listen, I just seem to long for more.
It's very nice, it tickles deep inside somewhere,
A most exciting part I didn't know was there.
ARNOLPHE [*aside*] Oh, what an inquisition! And for once it's true
For me to tell her, this will hurt me more than you!
[*to Agnes*]
It's clear that all his presents were a great success.
Apart from that, did he attempt the odd caress?
AGNES Oh, lots of times! He gently took my hands and arms,
And kissed them endlessly, and talked about their charms.
ARNOLPHE And didn't he try taking something else, Agnes?
[*She looks embarrassed*]
Ugh!
AGNES Er, he . . .
ARNOLPHE What did he? . . .
AGNES took . . .
ARNOLPHE Eh? . . .
AGNES my . . .
ARNOLPHE What?
AGNES Well, yes
He did, but I can't tell, because you'll be upset.
ARNOLPHE Not me.
AGNES It's true!
ARNOLPHE No, no!
AGNES You promise you won't fret?
ARNOLPHE I swear it.
AGNES Well, he took my . . . This'll make you cross!
ARNOLPHE No!
AGNES Yes!
ARNOLPHE No, no! Good grief! Look, I won't give a toss!
What did he take?
AGNES He took . . .

ARNOLPHE [*aside*] I'm suffering like hell!

AGNES He took my ribbon, that you gave me. Let me tell
You that I tried to stop him, but it was no good.

ARNOLPHE [*recovering his cool*] Well, never mind about the ribbon;
if he could,
Did he do more to you, than kiss your arms, and sigh?

AGNES Why? Are there other things that people like to try? . . .

ARNOLPHE It's time for you to learn that sometimes young men
come,
And try to give you presents. But, if you succumb,
And let yourself be coaxed, and give in to their art,
And let them kiss your hands and arms, and touch your heart,
You're guilty of a mortal sin, and you must die.

AGNES What, that's a sin, you say? How's that? Do tell me why.

ARNOLPHE I'll show you where it says so, printed on the page.
Behaviour like that puts heaven in a rage.

AGNES But what does it all mean, and why should heaven be cross?
It's much the most delicious thing I've come across.
I can't get over how delightful and how new
It is – I've learnt a secret that I never knew.

ARNOLPHE I know: what could be sweeter than those murmurings,
Those tender gestures, and those other charming things?
But they must be experienced in their own good time,
And people must get married. Then, it's not a crime.

AGNES So, if you're married, they don't count it as a sin?

ARNOLPHE That's right.

AGNES Can I get married? When can I begin?

ARNOLPHE It's what you want, and I want it as much as you,
Indeed, I've come back here today to marry you.

A Taste of Honey
Shelagh Delaney

First performed at the Theatre Royal, Stratford, London E15 in 1958 and transferred to Wyndham's theatre, London in 1959. Set in Manchester.

JO lives with her mother, Helen, in a run-down flat in Salford, Manchester. When Helen decides to remarry, JO is left on her own and consoles herself with JIMMIE (BOY), a young black naval rating. She becomes pregnant, but JIMMIE is by now overseas. She is cared for by GEOFF, a young effeminate art student, whom she invites to share the flat with her when his landlady throws him out. The baby is almost due when Helen returns home, her new husband having run off with a new 'bit of crumpet'. She drives GEOFF from the flat and settles in to look after JO and the new baby when it arrives.

In this scene we see JO and JIMMIE together for the first time. They are walking along the street and stop by the door to the flat.

Published by Methuen, London

Jo and her boyfriend, a coloured naval rating, walking on the street. They stop by the door.

JO I'd better go in now. Thanks for carrying my books.

BOY Were you surprised to see me waiting outside school?

JO Not really.

BOY Glad I came?

JO You know I am.

BOY So am I.

JO Well, I'd better go in.`

BOY Not yet! Stay a bit longer.

JO All right! Doesn't it go dark early? I like winter. I like it better than all the other seasons.

BOY I like it too. When it goes dark early it gives me more time for – [*He kisses her*]

JO Don't do that. You're always doing it.

BOY You like it.

JO I know, but I don't want to do it all the time.

BOY Afraid someone'll see us?

JO I don't care.

BOY Say that again.

JO I don't care.

BOY You mean it too. You're the first girl I've met who really didn't care. Listen, I'm going to ask you something. I'm a man of few words. Will you marry me?

JO Well, I'm a girl of few words. I won't marry you but you've talked me into it.

BOY How old are you?

JO Nearly eighteen.

BOY And you really will marry me?

JO I said so, didn't I? You shouldn't have asked me if you were only kidding me up. [*She starts to go*]

BOY Hey! I wasn't kidding. I thought you were. Do you really mean it? You will marry me?

JO I love you.

BOY How do you know?

JO I don't know why I love you but I do.

BOY I adore you. [*Swinging her through the air*]

JO So do I. I can't resist myself.

BOY I've got something for you.

JO What is it? A ring!

BOY This morning in the shop I couldn't remember what sort of hands you had, long hands, small hands or what. I stood there like a damn fool trying to remember what they felt like. [*He puts the ring on and kisses her hand*] What will your mother say?

JO She'll probably laugh.

BOY Doesn't she care who her daughter marries?

JO She's not marrying you, I am. It's got nothing to do with her.

BOY She hasn't seen me.

JO And when she does?

BOY She'll see a coloured boy.

JO No, whatever else she might be, she isn't prejudiced against colour. You're not worried about it, are you?

BOY So long as you like it.

JO You know I do.

BOY Well, that's all that matters.

155

JO When shall we get married?

BOY My next leave? It's a long time, six months.

JO It'll give us a chance to save a bit of money. Here, see . . . this ring . . . it's too big; look, it slides about . . . And I couldn't wear it for school anyway. I might lose it. Let's go all romantic. Have you got a bit of string?

BOY What for?

JO I'm going to tie it round my neck. Come on, turn your pockets out. Three handkerchiefs, a safety pin, a screw! Did that drop out of your head? Elastic bands! Don't little boys carry some trash. And what's this?

BOY Nothing.

JO A toy car! Does it go?

BOY Hm hm!

JO Can I try it? [*She does*]

BOY She doesn't even know how it works. Look, not like that. [*He makes it go fast*]

JO I like that. Can I keep it?

BOY Yes, take it, my soul and all, everything.

JO Thanks. I know, I can use my hair ribbon for my ring. Do it up for me.

BOY Pretty neck you've got.

JO Glad you like it. It's my schoolgirl complexion. I'd better tuck this out of sight. I don't want my mother to see it. She'd only laugh. Did I tell you, when I leave school this week I start a part-time job in a bar? Then as soon as I get a full-time job, I'm leaving Helen and starting up in a room somewhere.

BOY I wish I wasn't in the Navy.

JO Why?

BOY We won't have much time together.

JO Well, we can't be together all the time and all the time there is wouldn't be enough.

BOY It's a sad story, Jo. Once, I was a happy young man, not a care in the world. Now! I'm trapped into a barbaric cult . . .

JO What's that? Mau-Mau?

BOY Matrimony.

JO Trapped! I like that! You almost begged me to marry you.

BOY You led me on. I'm a trusting soul. Who took me down to that deserted football pitch?

JO Who found the football pitch? I didn't even know it existed. And it just shows how often you must have been there, too . . . you certainly know where all the best spots are. I'm not going there again . . . It's too quiet. Anything might happen to a girl.

BOY It almost did. You shameless woman!

JO That's you taking advantage of my innocence.

BOY I didn't take advantage. I had scruples.

JO You would have done. You'd have gone as far as I would have let you and no scruples would have stood in your way.

BOY You enjoyed it as much as I did.

JO Shut up! This is the sort of conversation that can colour a young girl's mind.

BOY Women never have young minds. They are born three thousand years old.

JO Sometimes you look three thousand years old. Did your ancestors come from Africa?

BOY No. Cardiff. Disappointed? Were you hoping to marry a man whose father beat the tom-tom all night?

JO I don't care where you were born. There's still a bit of jungle in you somewhere. [*A siren is heard*] I'm going in now, I'm hungry. A young girl's got to eat, you know.

BOY Honey, you've got to stop eating. No more food, no more make-up, no more fancy clothes; we're saving up to get married.

JO I just need some new clothes too. I've only got this one coat. I have to use it for school and when I go out with you. I do feel a mess.

BOY You look all right to me.

JO Shall I see you tonight?

BOY No, I got work to do.

JO What sort of work?

BOY Hard work, it involves a lot of walking.

JO And a lot of walking makes you thirsty. I know, you're going drinking.

BOY That's right. It's one of the lads' birthdays. I'll see you tomorrow.

JO All right. I'll tell you what, I won't bother going to school and we can spend the whole day together. I'll meet you down by that ladies' hairdressing place.

BOY The place that smells of cooking hair?

JO Yes, about ten o'clock.

BOY Okay, you're the boss.

JO Good night.

BOY Aren't you going to kiss me good night?

JO You know I am. [*Kisses him*] I like kissing you. Good night.
BOY Good night.
JO Dream of me.
BOY I dreamt about you last night. Fell out of bed twice.
JO You're in a bad way.
BOY You bet I am. Be seeing you!
JO [*as she goes*] I love you.
BOY Why?
JO Because you're daft.
[*He waves good-bye*]

VIOLA   DUKE ORSINO
young   young/middle-aged

Twelfth Night
William Shakespeare

First performed in 1600 and published in the First Folio of 1623.

A shipwreck brings VIOLA and her twin brother, Sebastian, to the coast of Illyria. The twins are separated in the wreck and VIOLA, believing her brother to be dead, disguises herself as a boy, 'Cesario'. She offers her services as page to ORSINO, Duke of Illyria. ORSINO is hopelessly in love with the Lady Olivia and employs VIOLA to deliver his love messages to her. Olivia is immediately attracted to VIOLA, who by now finds herself falling in love with ORSINO.

In this scene the lovesick ORSINO pours out his heart to VIOLA and asks if she has ever been in love.

Published by Penguin Popular Classics, London

DUKE Come hither boy, if ever thou shalt love
    In the sweet pangs of it, remember me;
    For such as I am, all true lovers are,
    Unstaid and skittish in all motions else,
    Save in the constant image of the creature
    That is belov'd. How dost thou like this tune?
VIOLA It gives a very echo to the seat
    Where Love is thron'd.
DUKE Thou dost speak masterly,
    My life upon't, young though thou art, thine eye
    Hath stay'd upon some favour that it loves:
    Hath it not boy?
VIOLA A little, by your favour.
DUKE What kind of woman is't?
VIOLA Of your complexion.
DUKE She is not worth thee then. What years i' faith?

VIOLA About your years my Lord.

DUKE Too old by heaven: let still the woman take
An elder than herself, so wears she to him;
So sways she level in her husband's heart:
For boy, however we do praise ourselves,
Our fancies are more giddy and unfirm,
More longing, wavering, sooner lost and worn,
Than women's are.

VIOLA I think it well my Lord.

DUKE Then let thy love be younger than thyself,
Or thy affection cannot hold the bent:
For women are as roses, whose fair flower
Being once display'd, doth fall that very hour.

VIOLA And so they are: alas, that they are so:
To die, even when they to perfection grow . . .

DUKE . . . Once more Cesario,
Get thee to yond same sovereign cruelty:
Tell her my love, more noble than the world
Prizes not quantity of dirty lands,
The parts that Fortune hath bestow'd upon her:
Tell her I hold as giddily as Fortune:
But 'tis that miracle and Queen of Gems
That nature pranks her in, attracts my soul.

VIOLA But if she cannot love you sir?

DUKE I cannot be so answer'd.

VIOLA Sooth but you must.
Say that some Lady, as perhaps there is,
Hath for your love as great a pang of heart
As you have for Olivia: you cannot love her:
You tell her so: must she not then be answer'd?

DUKE There is no woman's sides
Can bide the beating of so strong a passion,
As love doth give my heart: no woman's heart
So big, to hold so much, they lack retention.
Alas, their love may be call'd appetite,
No motion of the liver, but the palate,
That suffer surfeit, cloyment, and revolt,
But mine is all as hungry as the sea,
And can digest as much, make no compare
Between that love a woman can bear me,
And that I owe Olivia.

VIOLA Ay but I know.

DUKE What dost thou know?

VIOLA Too well what love women to men may owe:
  In faith they are as true of heart, as we.
  My father had a daughter lov'd a man,
  As it might be perhaps, were I a woman
  I should your Lordship.

DUKE And what's her history?

VIOLA A blank my Lord: she never told her love
  But let concealment like a worm i' th' bud
  Feed on her damask cheek: she pin'd in thought,
  And with a green and yellow melancholy,
  She sat like Patience on a Monument,
  Smiling at grief. Was not this love indeed?
  We men may say more, swear more, but indeed
  Our shows are more than will: for still we prove
  Much in our vows, but little in our love.

DUKE But died thy sister of her love my boy?

VIOLA I am all the daughters of my father's house,
  And all the brothers too: and yet I know not.
  Sir, shall I to this Lady?

DUKE Ay that's the theme,
  To her in haste: give her this jewel: say,
  My love can give no place, bide no delay.

Exeunt.

LINDY
40s
American

ADAM
40s
American

What the Night is For
Michael Weller

First performed at the Comedy Theatre, London in November 2002; set in a hotel room somewhere in a mid-sized Midwestern city.

Ten years after their affair in New York, two lovers – ADAM and LINDY – meet in a hotel room far from their homes. Both are now married, both have children and both have been wondering about the road not taken. What begins as a casual meal and an evening of catching up turns into a painful, sometimes funny, passionate and moving journey towards a moment that could change their lives forever.

In this opening scene LINDY and ADAM sit at a table eating a meal off a trolley with silver domes. She wears a tastefully stylish suit. ADAM is in tie and shirtsleeves, his jacket flung on the bed. Their mood is upbeat but a little shrill, each trying too hard to appear relaxed.

Published by Oberon Books, London

LINDY [*Guessing*] Millman? Hillman? Spillman, Spellman?
ADAM No.
LINDY Don't tell me, don't – Gellman. It was Gellman, right?
ADAM [*Having fun*] Nope.
LINDY He was an ear-nose-and-throat man –
ADAM Yes –
LINDY With a hideous wife.
ADAM Yes –
LINDY Isn't she the one who got drunk that time and said we should skip the book discussion and try group sex for a change?
ADAM That's the one.
LINDY His name was Gellman, I'm sure it was. That week was *Bonfire of the Vanities*.

ADAM Right book, wrong doctor. Gasarch. Dr Gasarch.

LINDY You know, I think you're right. He tried to grope me in the hallway my first night in the Book Circle. Well, doctors tend to be pretty biological on the whole. Don't you find?

ADAM [*Absurdly*] On the whole, absolutely.

LINDY [*Giggles*] Do you still see any of that bunch –

ADAM The Get-A-Life Culture Club?

LINDY Were they that pathetic?

ADAM Present company excepted.

LINDY Thank you.

ADAM Actually, I did ran into, was that obstetrics guy before your time – Dr Nicklaus? – vacation in Bora Bora at one of those, what are they, along the beach, open side thatched roof bar type things. He introduced me to a little dark haired cutie pie young enough to be someone he just delivered. His wife, he called her. The only good joke he ever told.

Lindy raises her champagne glass.

LINDY A toast; to the Book Circle.

ADAM And all that came of it! [*They click glasses*] Tattinger. You remembered.

LINDY I did? Oh . . . [*Then*] Remembered what?

ADAM My favourite champagne.

LINDY It's the little touches that do a perfect hostess make.

ADAM You *didn't* remember?

LINDY I'm sure I did. Sub-thing-a-mally. You've barely touched your fish.

ADAM Ditto your meat.

They take bites with awkward movements.

LINDY How is it?

ADAM My fish is fine. How's your meat?

LINDY Good, actually. Quite succulent and, um – tender – [*Hearing innuedo*] Oh dear, oh dear, Adam Penzius!

ADAM Your nose still turns red when you blush.

LINDY [*Busying herself with food*] So tell me all about yourself. How's your – you know, everything, life. You talk while *I* eat, then we'll switch round and I'll provide the ambient sound while you tackle your fish. How's that for a plan?

ADAM You haven't changed, Lindy.

LINDY It's a little warm though, isn't it? The hotel said they're testing a new air conditioning system . . . I'll open a window, why don't I do that, I'll just – Aren't you warm? Aren't I babbling?

ADAM I guess we're nervous.

LINDY A little.

ADAM Understandably.

LINDY I'll just/It *is* warm . . . [*She goes to the window*] [*Adam rises*] A boy was it? How old?

Adam almost calls her on this, then takes his jacket from the bed and removes some photos.

She turns.

They're awkwardly close in the middle of the room.

ADAM [*Showing her a photo*] Roo.

LINDY Roo? For Rudolf?

ADAM For Roo. As in 'Kanga and – .' From Winnie the Pooh. He curls up in my lap at breakfast, snuggles under my bathrobe like a baby kangaroo.

LINDY He's ten?

ADAM Clinging to his youth. Greg's his real name; Gregory.

So there they are, inches apart.

Lindy feels a wave of something and moves back to the table.

What were yours again?

LINDY Same as before; Doug and Bill.

ADAM [*Manly voice*] That's right; 'The Guys'.

He returns to the table and sits.

LINDY They are that, regular little jocks. Not so little now. Not completely jock, either, though Hugh does his best to push them that way. Football, baseball, basketball, anything with balls. *La Maison Testosterone*, that's what I call home. Is that your wife in the doorway?

He looks puzzled and half turns towards the door behind him.

Lindy grins, eyeing the photo beside Adam's plate.

In the picture.

Adam looks at the photo.

ADAM [*Surprised*] Oh, yes. Yes, that's – yes.

LINDY What's she like?

He studies the picture, sets it aside.

ADAM Oh, she's/she went back to work.

LINDY That's what she's *like*?

ADAM No, I mean – Career happens to be her focus right now, is all I – meant/ – when you asked –

He lifts the photo again, glances at it, puts it down.

Copyright Holders

The following have kindly granted us permission to reproduce copyright material:

Afterplay by Brian Friel
Reproduced by permission of
Faber and Faber Ltd.

Antigone by Sophocles,
translated by Don Taylor
Reproduced by permission of
Methuen Publishing Ltd.

Battle Royal by Nick Stafford
Reproduced by permission of
Faber and Faber Ltd.

Blithe Spirit by Noel Coward
Reproduced by permission of
Methuen Publishing Ltd.

Bondagers by Sue Glover
Reproduced by permission of
Methuen Publishing Ltd.

Borderline by Hanif Kureishi
Reproduced by permission of
Faber and Faber Ltd.

The Clink by Stephen Jeffries
Published by Nick Hern Books,
The Glasshouse, 49a Goldhawk
Road, London W12 8QP.

*Come Back to the 5 and Dime,
Jimmy Dean, Jimmy Dean* by
Ed Graczyk
Copyright © 1969, 1997 by Ed
Graczyk. *Caution*: Professionals
and amateurs are hereby
warned that 'Come Back to the
5 and Dime, Jimmy Dean,
Jimmy Dean' being fully
protected under the copyright
laws of the United States of
America, the British
Commonwealth countries,
including Canada, and the other
countries of the Copyright
Union, is subject to a royalty.
All rights, including
professional, amateur, motion
picture, recitation, public
reading, radio, television and
cable broadcasting, and the
rights of translation into foreign
languages, are strictly reserved.
Any inquiry regarding the
availability of performance
rights, or the purchase of
individual copies of the acting
edition, must be directed to
Samuel French Inc., 45 West 25
Street, NY, NY 10010 with
other locations in Hollywood
and Toronto, Canada.

Damsels in Distress: FlatSpin
and *GamePlan* by Alan
Ayckbourn
Reproduced by permission of
Faber and Faber Ltd.

Design for Living by Noel
Coward
Reproduced by permission of
Methuen Publishing Ltd.

Have You Seen Zandile? by
Gcina Mhlophe, Maralin
Vanrenen and Thembi Mtshali
Reproduced by permission of
Methuen Publishing Ltd.

The Jollies by Alan Ayckbourn
Reproduced by permission of
Faber and Faber Ltd.

A Laughing Matter by April De
Angelis
Reproduced by permission of
Faber and Faber Ltd.

Like a Virgin by Gordon Steel
Reproduced by permission of
Oberon Books.

Long Day's Journey into Night
by Eugene O'Neill
Reproduced by permission of
The Random House Group Ltd.

Love on the Dole by Ronald
Gow and Walter Greenwood
Reproduced by permission of
Film Rights Ltd. in association
with Laurence Fitch Ltd.

A Lovely Day Tomorrow by
Ellen Dryden
Taken from 'Harvest and Other
Plays' by Ellen Dryden,
published at £8.75 and available
from: First Writes Theatre
Company Ltd., Lime Kiln
Cottage, High Starlings,
Banham, Norwich NR16 2BS.
E-mail: ellen-don@first-
writes.co.uk. Performance rights
are protected by copyright.

Mindgame by Anthony
Horowitz
Reproduced by permission of
Oberon Books.

Mother Clap's Molly House by
Mark Ravenhill
Reproduced by permission of
Methuen Publishing Ltd.

Murmuring Judges by David
Hare
Reproduced by permission of
Faber and Faber Ltd.

Noises Off by Michael Frayn
Reproduced by permission of
Methuen Publishing Limited.

Oroonoko by Aphra Behn,
adapted by 'Biyi Bandele
Reproduced by permission of
Amber Lane Press Ltd.

A Prayer for Wings by Sean
Mathias
Reproduced by permission of
Amber Lane Press Ltd.

The extract by Alan Ayckbourn on pages 10–11 is reproduced by permission of Faber and Faber Ltd.

Every effort has been made to trace and acknowledge copyright holders. If any right has been omitted, the publishers offer their apologies and will rectify this in subsequent editions following notification.